Ben Townley. *Simon Cudby/Throttle Jockey*

Motocross and Off-road Motorcycle Setup Guide

By Mark Thompson

motorbooks

First published in 2010 by Motorbooks, an imprint of MBI Publishing Company, 400 First Avenue North, Suite 300, Minneapolis, MN 55401 USA

Motorbooks titles are also available at discounts in bulk quantity for industrial or sales-promotional use. For details write to Special Sales Manager at MBI Publishing Company, 400 First Avenue North, Suite 300, Minneapolis, MN 55401 USA.

To find out more about our books, visit us online at www. motorbooks.com.

Library of Congress Cataloging-in-Publication Data

Thompson, Mark, 1949-
  Motocross and off-road motorcycle setup guide / Mark Thompson.
    p. cm.
  Includes index.
  ISBN 978-0-7603-3596-3 (pbk. : alk. paper)
  1. Trail bikes--Maintenance and repair. I. Title.
  TL441.T535 2010
  796.7'56--dc22
                              2009039026

ISBN-13: 978-0-7603-3596-3

Editor: James Manning Michels and Jeffrey Zuehlke
Creative Director: Michele Lanci-Altomare
Design Manager: Jon Simpson
Designer: Wendy R. Lutge

Printed in China

On the cover: The next time you're at a pro race (if you haven't been to one, you're really missing out) take some time to watch the pro mechanics at work. You'll be amazed at how organized, methodical, and efficient they are when it comes to setup. *Steve Bruhn*

On the back cover: Ashley Fiolek. *Throttle Jockey*

Dedication: To the most important people in my life, and my personal life-long cheering section: My mother who first showed me the joy and importance of reading; to my wife Carole for her years of patience and support as I headed out the door each weekend for yet *another* race: and of course my wonderful daughter, Stephanie, who learned to ride dirt bikes when she was three and continues to remind me of why motorcycles have a big place in our lives.

About the Author: Mark Thompson long ago figured out he was put on earth to do two things: race motorcycles and write about racing. He's been at it ever since, having raced thousands of laps in a dozen states, along with riding many enduros and hare scrambles, as well as competing in ice races and some asphalt fun road races. Still an active racer after 40 years of motocross, he puts down laps in both modern and AHRMA vintage motocross. He's been a contributor to dozens of publications, editor of two motorcycle magazines, publisher of another, and managing editor for Readers' Digest The Family Handyman magazine. Mark is the author of MBI's **Motocross and Off-road Training Guide.** A lifetime jock, he's completed 10 marathons and hundreds of other running races. Originally from Wisconsin, he now lives in West Chester, Ohio where he owns Bear Motorsports, a motorcycle parts and accessories store. He can be reached at bearsports@gmail.com <mailto:bearsports@gmail.com> or his web site at www.bear-sports.com <http://www.bear-sports.com>.

Acknowledgments

No one writes a book by himself. I may be able to lay claim to most of the words, but that's just the beginning of a long process. Special thanks from my end go to: Jeff Zuehlke of Motorbooks for nursing this project along to completion; Ryan Weiser and Scott Louwis for their greatly appreciated help with photo shoots; loyal and royal assistant Maryann Turner; racing buddies Harry Gooch, Jim Denevan, Ted Simmons, and Woody Graves for ideas, insights, chapter reviews, pooh-poohing bad ideas, and serving as sounding boards and unpaid testers while keeping me in beer over the years we've raced together; James Dean of JD Jetting for advice; Shawn Rawlins of Works Connection for great products; Robert and Matt Davis of Throttle Jockey for ideas, support, and photos; Jody Olson of AirCell Fork Control System; Cole Townsend of Fasst Company; Nate at DirtTricks.com for the Iron Man sprockets; Ron Joynt of DecalWorks for help with the graphics portion; and apologies to anyone I've forgotten to include in this list.

Contents

Introduction

What This Book Is All About

Buying a dirt bike automatically makes you a member of a special fraternity. But unfortunately, nobody is going to show up in your garage to explain the secret handshake or answer the million or so "how do I do this?" questions you'll have. You have to learn pretty much everything on your own, the hard way, and make a lot of mistakes in the process. The purpose of this book is to show you the shortcuts, so you can flatten that learning curve. Important information has been condensed as much as possible into convenient bite-size chunks that will show you how to solve and avoid common problems.

All motorcycles, but especially dirt bikes, are design compromises. The manufacturers give you their best guess of an everyman's bike as a starting point and provide a lot of ways you can adjust and tune things to match your size, skills, personal preferences, and even your creativity. But because there are so many adjustable options, it's just as easy to make things worse rather than better—or be so overwhelmed with choices that you do nothing for fear of messing up your bike.

Here is a quick overview of some of what you can expect in these pages:

- Practical maintenance advice that applies to all dirt bikes of whatever type, size, and brand
- Shortcuts and tips that will save you time, money, and effort
- A very intentional focus on motocross bikes because they are at the cutting edge of the dirt bike world; other off-road bikes are based upon motocross bikes
- Suspension setup guidelines
- Jetting guidelines and identifying jetting problems
- How to properly set up any bike so that it fits the most important rider in the world: You
- Specific modifications and aftermarket products that anyone can install
- Race day problems and racing savvy
- Fuel and lubes, chains and sprockets, tires and wheels

In writing this book, my goal has been to keep the advice simple and to the point, so you can dive in at any point—even when you're in the middle of a project—and find out what you need to know, and then quickly get back to work.

Because motocross bikes are at the cutting edge of motorcycle design and development, what works in the intense environment of motocross racing also applies to other off-road bikes, from enduro/cross-country machines to the most docile dual-sport trail bike and even your kids' mini-bikes.

Please keep in mind that if your bike's manual says to do something one way and I say to do it another, trust the shop manual. This book has to be intentionally generic in nature, while your shop manual is about one very specific bike—yours. Your owner's manual and manufacturer's service manual cover the specifics of all major and minor maintenance jobs, and these manuals should always be your first references.

What This Book Is Not

While these pages contain some great repair and maintenance information, this is not a "how to repair every motorcycle" manual. That type of book doesn't exist and would be impossible to write, let alone keep current, given the fast pace of development in motorcycle technology.

I won't be attempting to turn you into a polished mechanic with this book—no book can do that. There are simply too many skills and too many specialized tools needed for the average rider to become an expert mechanic by flipping pages. However, there are several excellent books that will give you a solid grounding in the mechanical aspects of working on a dirt bike, notably the tuning books authored by Eric Gorr.

This also isn't a brand-specific book. The current, still-evolving, four-stroke era has the machines changing on an almost annual basis, and maintenance/repair routines change accordingly. Any model- or brand-specific book is already out of date by the time it's printed. If you're looking for a specific repair guide to a specific bike, your best bet is to purchase the manufacturer's service manual.

If you want to become a professional motorcycle mechanic, I recommend you enroll at one of the technical colleges and/or get a job at your favorite bike shop doing anything they'll let you do. Or you can start hanging around a professional mechanic and help him while absorbing all the repair tricks he demonstrates.

I hope that you find this book continuously useful, not just in setting up your current ride to match your needs, but also as a long term as a reference resource. Certainly, writing these pages reminded me that even after nearly 40 years of racing and involvement in the motorcycle industry as a motorcycle magazine editor, there are still topics where I'd rarely seen a good useful explanation of how to do things. I hope this book fulfills that purpose, gets you back on the track quicker, and enables you to ride faster and better. If so, then all the work was worth it.

Chapter 1
Tool Time

Dirt bikes and tools go together like beer and pizza. You won't be riding for long if you don't regularly spend some time with tools in your hands. While you can never be too rich, too thin, or have too many tools, filling your toolbox with the right items is more important than sheer quantity. If you are starting from scratch, here's what you need to equip your garage properly.

YOU NEED TWO

Get two toolboxes: One big main unit for the garage and a second traveling toolbox to take along when you go riding. The big main toolbox gets the good stuff, while the traveling toolbox is filled with low-cost but decent quality tools you can afford to lose or get rusty. Thanks to the big-box home improvement chains, you can now buy decent quality tools very cheaply.

The most important tool you can own: knowledge from the service manual.

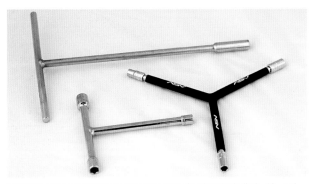

T-handles and a smaller version with three sizes of sockets (typically 8-, 10-, and 12mm sockets) speed up work and are must-have additions to your toolbox.

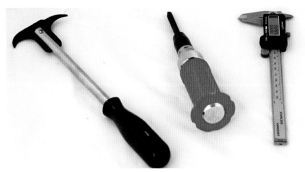

Not-so-special tools to have on hand. Left to right: A seal puller allows you to easily pop out engine seals without destroying surrounding surfaces or the seal; an impact driver will loosen stubborn screws without destroying them; and invest in a digital caliper to be sure you're measuring accurately because "close enough" seldom is.

For your garage toolbox, invest in a full-size mechanic's roll-around version with multiple drawers so you have enough room and can organize the contents. Fill it with good-quality tools and use magnetic labels on the drawers so you can find what you need when you need it.

What tools do you get? Here's a starting point.

HAND TOOLS AND EQUIPMENT

- Your most valuable tool is a service manual—the good, official book, direct from the factory. Buy one from the dealer or online. A service manual, used along with your owner's manual, is the most valuable tool you have, especially when you run into a head-scratching repair problem.
- A packaged set of quality metric sockets, both deep and regular length, plus ratchet handles in $1/2$-, $3/8$-, and $1/8$-inch drive sizes. Buying a packaged set is cheaper in the long run.
- T-handle wrenches, either a complete set or the most used sizes for your bike (typically 8, 10, 12, 13, and 14mm).
- A box-end wrench to fit the rear axle nut.
- A workbench. You can buy one or make one out of kitchen cabinets and a countertop. Make it sturdy, and the more built-in storage it has, the better.
- Dead blow hammer for those parts that need some persuasion to fit properly.

- Spring hook, because you never know when you'll need one, and you will be thanking your lucky stars you have it.
- Torque wrench. Plan on using it a lot, so make sure to buy a good one. In order to reduce weight, today's dirt bikes are using the smallest possible fasteners, and these must be torqued per the specs. You can break a lot of expensive motorcycle parts by over-tightening things.
- Measuring tools: A set of feeler gauges and a digital micrometer or calipers.
- A full set of screwdrivers.
- An ASV Y- or T-handle with the three most common socket sizes (8, 10, and 12mm).
- A full set of pliers, side-cutter, Vise-Grips, water pump pliers (ChannelLock), and similar holding/cutting pliers-style tools.
- A chain breaker. You can't easily cut a chain to size without one.
- Impact driver. You hit it with a hammer and it transmits that force into a twisting action that frees stubborn screws. Buy two, as you'll need one for the traveling toolbox as well.
- Bench vise with some removable padded jaws.

POWER TOOLS

- A good air compressor is sweet to have, and air tools have a lot of uses. While it is not essential, once you have air power on hand, you'll wonder how you survived without it.
- Electric staple gun. It lets you easily install replacement seat covers.
- A bench grinder is always used, as is an electric drill.
- A power washer, either electric or gas. The electrics are lighter and less hassle, but the gas versions have more power. See the section on correctly using a power washer.
- A Dremel Moto-Tool. You'll constantly find uses for one.

TIRE-CHANGING TOOLS

- Get real tire irons (also called tire spoons), at least 10 inches long. You need leverage. Two are the bare minimum, but more are better.

A good accurate torque wrench is something you should be using frequently.

A tire-changing stand seems like a luxury until you discover how much it simplifies tire-changing chores. This one cost me about $100 and has earned its keep many times over.

CHEAP THREAD LOCK

To guarantee that nuts and bolts don't loosen but are easy to remove when necessary, use a healthy dab of GE Silicone Seal (the same stuff you use around the bathtub). Besides being cheaper than the usual thread-locking compounds, the clear silicone keeps the threads clean.

You can have a bike stand where you have to muscle the bike up onto the stand, or you can get a foot-operated lift stand like this.

Intended for the garage only, a hydraulic bike lift like this costs about $200 and provides a wide stable platform for the bike, while allowing you to raise the bike to a more comfortable working height.

- One long tire iron. These big boy 16- or 18-inch numbers provide the leverage you need for a really stubborn tire.
- Motion Pro Bead Popper. This hard plastic wedge will unseat the most stubborn tire bead without damaging your wheel.
- Valve core remover. Get a couple of these as they're small and tend to disappear.
- A portable tire-changing stand will speed up tire changes while saving you a lot of frustration, sore knees, and skinned knuckles. Stands let you apply enough leverage to get that stubborn rubber donut under control. You can find stands for home use for about $100 on up, and they're worth it. If you're bucks-down, get a metal garbage can or 55-gallon metal drum (empty) to use as a make-shift tire-changing stand.
- Tire-valve puller. These clever little tools let you easily pull the tube's valve stem up and through that tiny little hole in the rim.

BIKE STANDS

- A large and stable bike stand for your wrenching is a necessity. Personally, I prefer the lift stand variety rather than the heave-it-up-and-pray stands, but it's your choice (and back).
- A high-rise hydraulic stand is good to have and is preferable over a simple bike stand. Hydraulic stands are strictly for shop use due to their weight. These stands save your back because they will raise a bike to a comfortable working height. You can find these for $120 on up.
- If you want to spend the big bucks for a table-style work stand, keep in mind that you need to be able to remove the bike's wheels regularly, and some of these stands aren't very convenient in this situation. These work stands are the least useful for a dirt biker.

OTHER GOOD STUFF

- Have enough light. The more light you can throw on your work area, the quicker the work will go. Hang some shop halogen lights or 8-foot fluorescents. Have at least one portable light that you can bring to bear on a specific part of the bike.
- Buy one of those million-candlepower portable spotlights for $20. These are lifesavers when looking for a dropped part that's rolled away, reading the tiny etching on a carb jet, or to get enough light into a dark recess of the engine.
- A graduated (in cc's and ounces) plastic measuring beaker. The baby section of most stores will have one.
- A rolling mechanic's seat. It saves your back and your knees.
- A lighted magnifying glass. Any office supply store will have these. It makes it easy to see the numbers on carb jets and other tiny parts.

THE ART OF POWER WASHING

The power washer is one of those wonderful inventions that also can cause major problems. Like any tool, it has to be used the right way. Here's how:

- Loosen up the mud and grime by hosing down the bike. At this point you just want things wet and soft.
- Spray on a cleaner such as Shout or a bike-specific product on oily spots, under fenders, your seat, and so on. Give it a few minutes to work its magic.
- Crank up the power washer and adjust the nozzle pressure to the **lowest** setting that effectively removes the dirt and mud. Some power washers can deliver a stream that will etch concrete. You definitely don't want to use that much pressure on your bike.
- Be careful around suspension parts, chains, seals, and bearings. You can literally blast the protective grease out of them. Think about where the water is going and how it could do more damage than good.

- Be careful around decals and numbers, unless they're the backside-printed type. If a corner of the decal is sticking up, chances are you'll blow it right off the bike.
- If cleaning between motos and you only have a limited amount of water on hand, focus on getting the tires and bottoms of the fenders free of mud. Don't worry about getting it pretty; just get those heavy clumps of mud off the bike.
- Use the power washer sparingly because while it does a spectacular job of cleaning things, all that high-pressure water is also going to increase your maintenance costs.
- Use WD-40 or a blowgun attachment to an air compressor to drive water out of the chain and other components.
- Start the bike up and let it warm up while you towel it off.

There's a right way and a wrong way to use a power washer. Most people do it the wrong way. Use the least power and the least water while keeping the wand away from suspension pieces, bearings, and seals.

Get off your knees and onto a mechanic's roller seat. Your back will say "thanks, dude!"

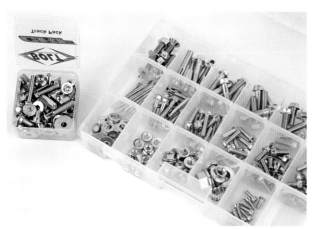

One of the laws of nature is that any dropped fastener will disappear forever if it happens at night when all the stores and shops are closed. To prevent this, have a selection of fasteners for your bike on hand and you'll never have to worry about this again. Some of these kits come matched to your make/model.

- A parts washer, if you have room. It simplifies and confines the mess when degunking parts.
- A boxed set of spare fasteners in a variety of sizes to fit your bike. These are life- and money-savers, especially if you find yourself doing a late-night pre-ride repair.
- A fire extinguisher and a decent first-aid kit can literally be lifesavers in the garage.
- Shelving for parts, spares, fluids, manuals, and your riding gear. Get the sturdy stuff.
- Comfort items: music system, TV, a chair or two, a refrigerator to hold cold drinks, etc.

SPECIALTY TOOLS

- A Motion Pro steering stem wrench is one of those tools you'll only use rarely, but when you need it you'll be patting yourself on the back that you had the smarts to buy one.

USING, NOT ABUSING, THREAD-LOCK COMPOUND

Myth-busting time. Thread-locking compound, such as Loctite, is not something you need to use constantly, or much at all, on your race bike. In fact, if you're using a lot of thread-lock on fasteners, you're making them *more* likely to loosen and get false torque readings.

Pro mechanics use assembly lube on clean fasteners and then torque to spec, and rarely use Loctite. It only gets applied in critical areas and never on frequently removed parts. Here's what you need to know:

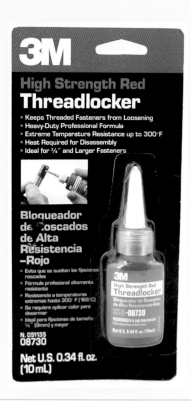

- Avoid using it on frequently removed fasteners unless you take the time to completely clean off the old thread-lock compound. Otherwise, you will get a false torque reading and you're making the fastener more likely to loosen.

- Never use it on the aluminum steering stem nut.

- Never use it on radiator shroud fasteners or any fastener that threads into a metal insert in a plastic part.

- Be sure you're using the correct type— and there are many—of thread-locking compounds based on the application and the size of the fastener. Refer to the service manual, and if no thread-lock is specified, then don't use it.

- If you use permanent thread-lock, you will need heat from a butane torch to loosen the fasteners. Don't use it any place you can't heat it up as necessary.

- Use Loctite primer on stainless-, plated-, or anodized-steel threads or else the Loctite won't work.

- More is not necessarily better. Use two or three drops on fasteners up to 8mm, and a couple more for larger ones.

- Clean off old thread-lock with a wire brush, acetone, or contact cleaner.

- Thread-lock typically takes 24 hours to cure. Therefore it's worthless to apply a few minutes before going riding.

- Don't use thread-lock on shock bolts that thread directly into the frame or on bolts that thread into a suspension link.

- Learn how to install safety wire if you have fasteners that consistently come loose or make you worry.

It might surprise you to learn that thread-locking compounds are rarely required by the manufacturer and that overuse or improper use can actually make the fasteners more likely to loosen.

- Sag scale. These simplify shock preload measuring. Some versions fold in half to fit in your toolbox. ASV and Pro Motion make ones that you can use solo.
- A Fasst Company spoke torque wrench takes the guesswork out of wheel and spoke maintenance. Don't try to do it by feel and sound. Instead, just tighten the spoke until you hear and feel the click of the torque setting. The spoke is now properly tightened without any guesswork.
- Fork cap wrench. It will fit the large flat hex caps found on most modern MX bikes.
- If you're going to be doing any of your own suspension work, plan on getting the fork cap wrench, cartridge rod holder, fork seal drivers to fit (these can also be made from PVC pipe), and other specialized tools.
- Safety-wire pliers. These cut and tighten safety wire in one simple operation.
- Steahly engine lockup tool. This hard plastic slug screws into the spark plug hole of a two stroke motor to lock it up so you can remove a bolt on a flywheel or clutch. Cheap ($10) and priceless.

When a part gets lost or you need to see deep within an assembly, the million-candlepower spotlights are the solution.

LABEL YOUR TOOLS

An easy way to label your tools, especially sockets, is with a Sharpie permanent marker and then coat it with clear nail polish. It won't last forever, but it's cheap and easily renewed. If your racing buddies regularly mooch your tools, put your name on the tools or spray paint them some hideous color so they're easy to identify.

Having a hard time reading the socket sizes? Use a Sharpie to make them easy to read. Borrow some clear nail polish from your wife and use it to protect the new labels.

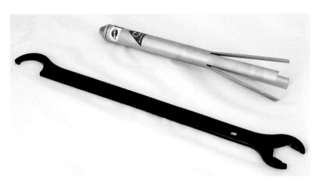

You need a stem wrench to loosen the big nut that holds the steering stem in place. If you have to replace the steering head bearings because you didn't bother to grease them (you dummy!), you will need the Park Tools steering stem bearing tool.

Simplify reassembly and avoid problems. Whenever possible, after you take out a fastener, lightly reinstall it so it's there when it's time to put things back together. Don't just throw everything in a box and hope you can sort them out later.

- Park Tools steering stem bearing remover. It is the quick and easy way to remove and reinstall steering stem bearings. It's a lifesaver.
- If you're going to be doing your own engine work, you'll need a fairly comprehensive selection of tools. Your shop manual will show you what tools you need, including the specialized ones. Your dealer can order the special tools for your bike.

RACE DAY TOOLBOX AND SPARES

Riders tend to have two approaches to their race day tools and spares. Either they bring everything they could possibly need, which is nice if you have the room, or they use the minimalist approach, where they hope for no mechanical emergencies and/or the generosity of their buddies and pit neighbors. Of course they also risk ending up with a reputation as a mooch.

There's a third method: planning ahead. This requires putting some thought into it and creating a separate, race day–only traveling toolbox filled with enough of the right tools. You back that up with a separate plastic storage box containing the fluids and spares that match your bike and the problems you're likely to encounter. Planning gives you a lighter toolbox and less to haul around.

Stock the race day toolbox with spare tools or buy a packaged set of sockets, wrenches, and screwdrivers at one of the big-box stores. Get tools that aren't cheap, fall-apart junk, but that also aren't so expensive that you care (much) if you lose them or they get rusty from being out in the rain. Below is a list of what to stash in the race day tool and spares box:

GET MAGNETIC

Use a magnetic bowl or mat to keep track of fasteners when working on your bike. The magnetic mat should be in your race day toolbox, as it folds flat and keeps you from losing that gotta-have-it screw when doing a repair in the pits. Keep in mind, however, that not all the fasteners and spacers are steel.

TRAVELING TOOLS AND SPARES

- An accurate tire pressure gauge (not one of those stick things) and a bicycle tire pump. A cheapo tire pump will work as well as the expensive one from the bicycle store.
- A set of deep sockets and at least one ⅜-inch ratchet handle.
- A small tape measure with metric dimensions for checking suspension sag (see Chapter 4).
- A set of T-handle wrenches in sizes to fit your bike. This is the one item you usually can't find cheap at one of the home improvement megastores.
- An ASV Y-handle tool with three socket sizes. These little tools are great timesavers because most race bikes rely on just three sizes of fasteners for 90 percent of the bike. Having them all on one tool means you don't waste any time searching for the right sizes, which is great when your class is being called to the start line and you find out your levers are in the wrong position or a body panel is loose.
- Dead blow hammer to nudge reluctant parts into place.
- Two 10-inch tire irons and a valve core remover.

- Rolling drift pin. It's useful for prying, aligning parts, adjusting the sag, and whenever else you need a big, sturdy punch.
- Screwdriver set, including a couple with long handles, in both slot and Phillips varieties.
- Superglue grip glue. It lets you install a new grip that will be tight and ready to go in a matter of minutes.
- Metric Allen wrenches, preferably T-handle style, but the folding set is okay if nothing else is available. Only take along the sizes that fit your bike.

TOOLBOX NAVIGATION

When you've got a lot of tools, remembering which drawer something is in can be a hassle. You can purchase preprinted toolbox labels or make your own with strips of magnetic tape that have a write-on surface. Just use a Sharpie permanent marker to write the label and scissors to cut the label to fit.

SAVING MONEY ON DEALER REPAIRS

Sometimes it makes more sense to pay someone else to do the work. Here are some ways to cut your costs:

- Many dealers offer a discount on parts and accessories if you're a member of the AMA or other racing organization. Ask about this.
- Schedule your work during the off-season, especially the slowest months.
- Show up with a clean bike. Mechanics hate being handed a dirty bike, and they'll charge you to clean it.
- Show up with plastic panels and other parts already removed to save the mechanic some work time and you some money.
- Write out what problems you're having and what you want done. Be clear and concise, but don't try to analyze exactly what's wrong—leave that to the mechanics. Clear information prevents confusion and makes sure the problems you want fixed are looked at. Have this stapled to the work order so the mechanic can refer to it.

So that I don't forget to bring along something essential, I keep a plastic storage box packed with my race day spares, lubes, and necessities. It's ready to throw in the truck anytime I want to go ride.

- A Vise-Grips pliers or two (one needle-nose, one larger blunt-nose).
- Something for scraping mud off the bike. Use stiff plastic rather than a metal putty knife. You might be able to find a specialized mud-scraping tool that MSR and others sell.
- A selection of nuts, bolts, and washers that fit your bike, especially the plastic pieces. You can either create a package tailored to your bike with a trip to the local hardware store's metric fastener section or buy prepackaged fastener sets from your dealer. If you're going the hardware store route, make sure it's marked 8.8, which is the middle grade in metric fasteners and the same pitch as what your bike uses. A search on eBay will show you some prepackaged fastener kits for specific bike models that are a good investment.
- A spare chain master clip and end plate.
- A spare shift lever. See Chapter 4 on setting up the bike to properly fit you and why you should replace the stock shifter with an aftermarket unit that fits your boot.
- You don't need to take along spare clutch or front brake levers if you replace the stockers with folding (pivoting) levers from companies such as ASV, the original inventors of pivoting levers.
- Flat tire aerosol inflator. It's a quick fix when you don't have time to change the tube.
- The last good used tube(s) from your most recent tire change; one for each end.
- The lubes and liquids you're likely to need.
- Some Nitrile gloves, hand cleaner, and packaged cleaning towels or clean shop rags.

GARAGE SUPPLIES

- Nitrile gloves. These thin blue plastic gloves aren't latex and are durable enough for garage work while thin enough to allow plenty of feel. They protect your hands from the toxic chemical irritants and messes that come with working on a bike. The fit and feel are excellent—if you have the right size, you can pick up fasteners easily—and they last quite a while without tearing. You can buy a box of 50 or 100 at home improvement stores for $10. Long-time mechanics develop a sensitivity to many of the caustic chemicals used around the shop, and these gloves help keep you from developing health problems. Spraying brake cleaner on bare skin is as bad as drinking the stuff, so wear these gloves for your own health's sake.
- Anti-seize. Use this thick, silvery liquid to keep fasteners from corroding and welding themselves together. It is especially useful on things like chain adjuster bolts threaded into aluminum swingarms.
- Assembly lube. This thick lube, when used on a clean fastener, ensures that you're getting an accurate torque reading.
- Grip glue. Get the real stuff and not some homemade solution. See Chapter 5 for more on this. For some reason, a lot of dirt bike riders experiment with goofball ways to attach grips. Forget that. Use proper grip glue and always have some on hand so it's there when you need it.
- Maxima SC1 silicone detailer. After washing the bike, the last step is shining up the plastic with this stuff. Do your spraying outside with a breeze because the fumes are tough on your lungs. Mop N Glow also works.
- Dry erase board and markers. Put a board up in your garage and use it to record things you need to do, like the last oil change, how much oil to use after changes, race dates, and other info you need to know.
- There are potent concentrated cleaners available at the hardware store, but these products can also etch aluminum or dull plastic even when diluted. Use a laundry spot cleaner like Shout, which cuts dirt but won't damage metal and costs less. Soak the bike down first to loosen dried mud, then spray Shout on the bike and let it soak in. Using Shout gets the bike just as clean as using a power washer but without the damaging high pressure water blasts. The bike also comes away smelling clean. If you have access to hot water through a hose connection, use it.

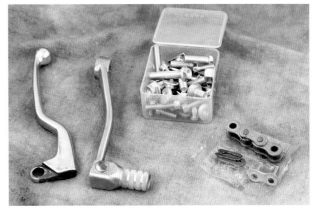

Spares to always have along: shift lever, chain master clip, and some common fasteners. You'll be glad you had them along.

Almost every aerosol product we use in working on our bikes is toxic or potentially damaging to your skin and health. Nitrile gloves are much tougher than latex, fit tightly, and protect your hands. Buy them at any hardware store.

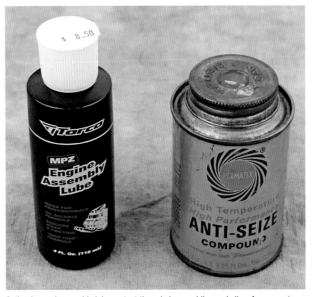

Anti-seize and assembly lube protect threaded assemblies and allow for accurate torque readings.

Chapter 2
Basic Bike Setup

Whether you buy new or used, taking care of the setup procedures described here will pay off with a more reliable motorcycle and one you can feel confident is working the way it was designed to perform.

As tempting as it is to jump on your new purchase and go pound some laps, it's better to take the time to properly prep and double-check the dealer's work or the previous owner's maintenance skills. Here are the steps, starting with a new bike fresh and sweet-smelling from your dealer.

NEW BIKE PREP:
WHAT THE DEALER DID AND DIDN'T DO

Some dealers are very good at new bike prep, some are okay, and some dump the setup chores off on the lowest-paid and least-skilled kid in the back room. Usually, you won't know which situation you're facing, so it's probably best to be a little paranoid.

Before you load your new bike and drive off, do a walk-around with the salesman or preferably the service manager.

Ask questions and take notes if necessary. Look for any obvious problems. Be sure you receive the owner's manual, tool kit, and all your purchase information—the manual is always included in the price. Have the service manager demonstrate the proper starting routine, then you try it. Ask about engine warmup time, break-in, and any other advice he has to offer on taking care of your new ride. A good service manager knows what things to keep an eye on. If there are obvious problems with the bike, now is the time to have them addressed before you leave the dealer.

Finally, buy a couple quarts of the recommended oil at the dealer, an oil filter, and a spare air filter (OEM or aftermarket), as you're going to be doing an oil change almost immediately.

BE "OLD SCHOOL" ABOUT NEW BIKES

A new dirt bike is a wonderful thing, and understandably your first reaction is going to be to want to pour some gas in the tank and put it through its paces. That's human nature, but it's absolutely the wrong thing to do. Be old school instead.

While today's dirt bikes are very reliable and so competent straight out of the box that many people treat them like an appliance, if you go back a few years, the reverse was true.

Back in the days of open-face helmets, Jofa mouth guards, and European race bikes that weren't sheathed in layers of plastic, a new dirt bike was an unreliable, cantankerous, unfinished kit-bike project that required work before you rode or even started it the first time. You knew better (or soon learned the hard way) than to go riding without first doing the things that would enable it to survive. Fast-forward a couple decades, and while today's machines are far more race-ready out the door, if you want to have the maximum performance and the fewest problems from the abuse it's going to experience, then you need to prep the bike right at the beginning.

Sad but true, the first thing you should do when you get your new bike is put it up on the bike stand and open the toolbox. Knowing that a lot of people can't resist riding first and wrenching later, here's the *minimum* preflight check you need to do, followed by the old school prep.

Set the sag on a new bike as your first step in getting the suspension set up properly. You don't need anything more than a helper and measuring tape (metric preferred).

Brand-new suspensions need a couple hours of riding time to break in, so hold off on playing with the clickers a while.

Before riding the first time, spray brake cleaner on each rotor and wipe clean with a clean rag. This removes the anti-corrosion coating.

MINIMUM PREFLIGHT CHECK

A bike is only new once. One ride in the dirt and everything changes. Graphics and plastic get scratched, a crash will tweak controls or bend parts, the pipe collects dings along with a baked-dirt hue, metal pieces start to rub against each other, and mud and dirt collect in areas that are impossible to clean.

If you absolutely cannot wait to ride, then at least do the following things FIRST:

- Get out the owner's manual and start READING it. Note the emphasis. READ the manual, don't just skim through it. There's a lot of good information on tap. Find out what the manufacturer advises for break-in procedures, first (baseline) suspension settings, proper lubricants, and any warnings.
- Check all fluid levels and top off as necessary. Never trust the dealer or factory to have the right fluid level. Check it yourself.
- Recheck fluid levels after the first 15 minutes of riding.
- Check the air filter to make sure it's properly oiled and seated. It might have been sitting there for the last 10 months. If it doesn't feel tacky to the touch,

it's not going to stop fine dust. If in doubt, remove and re-oil.
- Check lever position, adjustment, and free-play.
- Depending on your physique and preferences, you may want or need to change the handlebars immediately. New bars also mean new grips, so use super glue grip adhesive so it will dry quickly.
- Adjust the chain slack to spec and make sure the chain adjusters are correctly aligned.
- Check tire pressure when you get to the riding area (see Chapter 3).
- Set the sag. See Chapter 4 for the drill.
- Check and "center" the suspension clickers to their base settings, per the owner's manual. Suspensions need time to break in, so generally it's best to leave the clickers alone for the first hour of riding. At this point, you just want to be sure that the settings are at their baseline.
- Think seriously about doing the old school setup steps described next instead of going riding.
- At each break from riding, recheck fluids, check spoke tension, and look for problems.

OLD SCHOOL BIKE PREP

It's only new once, and when it's still virgin is the perfect time to make sure things are *exactly* how you want them.

While the steps listed here require a lot of time—easily a solid day in the garage—what you get back is confidence that your bike is properly prepped, while also acquiring some intimate mechanical knowledge which makes adjustments and problem-solving easier. You'll also have a better first ride/first race experience and quite likely a higher resale value down the road. Set aside the time to do the following:

- Put it up on the stand and start READING the manual. Make notes about products to buy, adjustments to make, current settings as delivered, and create a Cheat SheetZ for your bike (see the sample on page 24).
- Check all the fluid levels and top off or replace as needed.
- Center the suspension clickers to the baseline settings, per the manual. Suspensions need time to break in, so you want your first couple of hours of riding time to be at the base setting based on your weight. The manual has instructions.
- Set the sag. See Chapter 4 for the drill.
- Check the air filter and re-oil if necessary. You might want to re-oil it even if it doesn't seem necessary, since you have no idea how long the filter has been sitting there.
- Do anything else the manual "suggests" as race preparation, even if you're never going to enter a race.
- Now is the time for whatever modifications you're going to make. If you know you're going to change the bars, pegs, pipe, graphics, and whatever else, have those parts on hand. Your dealer will probably cut you a nice discount if you purchase these items the same time you pick up the bike. Heck, work it into the sales contract if necessary.

- Remove any parts that you're going to replace and put them in a plastic storage bin for protection. This is your personal spare parts department, and these parts come in handy when it's time to sell your bike and you want to migrate the aftermarket goodies to another bike or sell them separately.
- Disassemble and grease the rear suspension linkage and swingarm. Put plenty of grease on all the bearings because the factories tend to go light on the lubes. Use the specified type of lubricant listed in the manual and work it into the bearings. See Chapter 4 for details.
- When reassembling fasteners, put a dab of assembly lube on the threads so they reinstall easily and will give you an accurate torque reading (you DO have a torque wrench and you do USE IT, right?).
- Do the same to the steering head bearings when disassembling, greasing, and reassembling. Tighten the steering stem nut so the bars turn freely but don't flop from side to side. Be sure to reinstall the front wheel per the manual so the wheel is properly centered in the clamps.
- While you have the rear suspension off, now is a good time to make any changes to the carb since you have better access with half the bike apart. Change the jetting to what works in your area or via one of the jetting kits (JD Jetting is our preference). See Chapter 8.
- Unless you know exactly what needs to be done, it's better to ride first and let the suspension have time to break in before sending it off for changes.
- Install an hour meter so you know *exactly* how much time you have on the engine.
- Install aftermarket armor (Works Connection, etc.), such as glide plates, radiator guards, and so on. Radiators cost about $300 each, so install radiator braces. They won't

Thoroughly grease all parts of the rear suspension and steering stem.

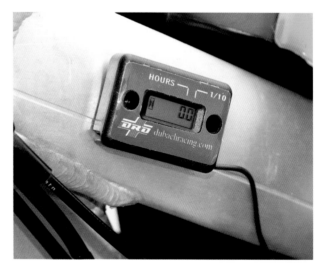

An hour meter lets you track actual time on the motor and reminds you of maintenance schedules.

JD Jetting kits are tailored for your bike and area/altitude. They are a quick way to clean, precise, correct jetting.

Cheap insurance: Put some Never-Seez on the chain adjuster bolts before threading them back into the swingarm. It keeps the adjusters from chemically corroding and welding themselves to the aluminum.

absolutely save the radiator in all crashes (nothing will), but they're cheap insurance that keeps a simple tip-over from costing you hundreds of dollars.

- Add any billet bling that catches your eye.
- Replace the stock plastic throttle tube with a billet version or one of the billet-and-bearing styles. The stock throttle tube goes into your spare parts bin.
- Take out the chain adjusters and brush some Never-Seez on the threads and reinstall. This will keep them from corroding and seizing in the swingarm, something that will cause you considerable grief.
- Install your favorite handlebar, grips, and any other control items that help adjust the cockpit to your personal dimensions (see Chapter 4).
- Since you've been taking things off and on, make sure cables are routed correctly and there's no binding when turning the handlebars lock to lock. Your manual will have the routing details.
- Spray brake cleaner on both discs and wipe clean with a towel. New discs come with an anti-corrosion coating that ends up on your brake pads and decreases braking efficiency if not removed first.
- If you often ride in extremely wet and muddy conditions, take the electrical connections apart, apply dielectric grease to prevent corrosion, reassemble, and wrap with electrical tape.
- Break out your torque wrench and check all critical fasteners, starting with engine mounts, suspension pieces, and so on. Apply thread-locking compound if called for in the manual, but otherwise avoid it. (See Chapter 1 for using/not abusing thread-lock.)
- Install new graphics, plastic, and other personal touches (see Chapter 6).
- Stock pegs are typically dull and don't grip boots well, probably to keep the manufacturers' lawyers happy. Put an edge to the pegs' teeth with a triangular-shaped file so they provide some bite.

When you're done, pat yourself on the back, take a well-deserved break, and then do a quick double-check of your work to be sure everything has been properly tightened and all fasteners are back in place. You're ready to ride!

USED DIRT BIKE PREP: WHAT YOU NEED TO DO

When you buy a used dirt bike, you're tiptoeing blindfolded through a minefield. That said, there are also some great bargains out there. A lot of bikes see little use once the new owner discovers riding in the dirt isn't as simple as it looks on TV or a video game. The flipside is that these newbie owners are the ones most likely ignoring basic maintenance and then claiming in their ads that the bike was "never raced." (See the used bike buyer's guide later in this chapter for tips, some of which I confess to having learned the hard way.)

BREAK IT IN RIGHT

As with religion, everybody has an opinion when it comes to breaking in a new or rebuilt motor. Some tout a "full race, ride it like you stole it" approach under the theory that's how it will be ridden, while others suggest a more measured and time-proven method. The race team factory mechanics may advise one thing and the dealer another. The race mechanics, however, are going to be rebuilding that engine soon anyhow, so break-in is the least of their worries.

The factories are the ultimate judge and this is what they advise:

- With the sag set and all fluids topped off and the brake rotors cleaned of anti-corrosion residue, ride for 15 minutes at a moderate but not all-out pace. Don't over-rev and don't lug the engine.
- Put the bike up on a stand and let it cool completely (30 minutes). Use this time to check the spokes, recheck fluids, adjust the chain, look for loose parts, etc.

- Ride for another 15 minutes, then repeat the cool-off and check-it-over routine.
- At this point you can choose to either announce the break-in complete or repeat the 15 minutes/cool-off process until you've put in one hour of riding.
- After the first hour or two of riding, drain the engine oil and install fresh oil and maybe a filter if you're the belt-and-suspenders type.
- You're now good to go.

The Used Dirt Bike Setup Checklist

Get a manual, preferably the correct owner's manual or factory shop manual. At the minimum, get one of the Clymer or Haynes books. Buy manuals online (eBay is a good place to find them) or at your dealer. One clue to an abused used bike is when the seller doesn't have a manual. If that's the case, be very cautious. READ the manual while doing the following tasks:

- With the bike on a stand, start taking things off and checking what you see against what the manual lists, especially noting the modifications. Make a list of things you need to do and purchase.
- Assume the worst. Be a lemon-sucking, insanely paranoid, and cranky pessimist. Double-check anything the seller claimed was done. New spark plug? Check it yourself. Fresh top end? Ditto. Fresh oil and filter? Hah! Brother, there's only one way to be sure and that's to check it yourself. Assume the seller was either wrong, forgetful, or flat out lied to you. He may also

have been honest and a really nice guy but the world's worst mechanic.

- Do the full old school bike prep list detailed earlier. Go from one end of the bike to the other, checking, adjusting, lubricating, replacing, and repairing components. This will take time and some cash outlay, but it'll be time and money well spent.
- Drain out the old gas and dispose of it using the method described later in this chapter or take it to your local hazardous waste disposal operation (go to www. earth911.com to find the closest one). Depending on how long it has been sitting, you may also want to remove the petcock and clean out the fuel filter. Remove the float bowl bolt on the carb and let the old fuel drain out. Clean and reinstall.
- If it's a thumper, find the breather tube and drain out the gunk that has accumulated.
- Find out the jetting specs. Remove the carb, clean the jets thoroughly with carb cleaner, and note the jetting specs

(text continues on page 26)

Air filters aren't diamonds. They wear out. Have more than one and rotate usage.

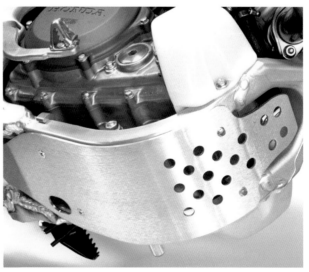

Protect the underside of your engine with a good glide plate. If you ride in very rocky areas, a full skid plate that also protects the frame is cheap insurance.

CHEAT SHEETZ®

Who has time to flip through a big owner's manual when all you want to know is a couple of quick settings? That's why you need Cheat SheetZ®. It summarizes the standard and modified settings you use most often.

A Cheat SheetZ is priceless when your class is being called to the start line and you know you need to change the clickers a few notches. But which way and which adjustment? Your Cheat SheetZ will tell you.

Below is the Cheat SheetZ I use for one of my bikes. I have it laminated in clear plastic and carry it in my gone-racing toolbox for quick and easy reference. As I make changes, I note them on the Cheat SheetZ to remind me of what I did, why, when, and where.

Another approach is to use a racer's logbook—any notebook—to record changes, track conditions that work with various setups, jetting, etc. Pro mechanics have relied on logbooks for years so they can keep track of what setups work for what tracks.

On page 25 is a blank version that you can copy out of this book to create a Cheat SheetZ for your own bike.

2006 CRF450 Cheat SheetZ®

Oil	Engine	660 cm no filter 690 cm w/ filter	SG or higher JASO T903 MA ProHonda GN4, HP4, HP4M
	Trans	590 cm	SG or higher, as above ProHonda GN4 or HP4
Race Sag	100mm	Mud: 5/10mm **less sag** Sand: **increase sag** 5/10mm	Mud: stiffer on compression/rebound Sand: stiffer on rebound, **maybe** compression
Plug		NGK IFR8H11	ND VK24PRZ11
Tires	Front Rear	80/100-21 110/90-19	Michelin MS-3
Chain	520	114 links	
Sprockets	13/48	3.692 ratio	
Jetting	#168 MJ #42 SJ Clip: 4th notch	Cold: Go **Richer** Very Dry Air: Go **Richer** High Humidity/Raining: Go **Leaner** High Altitude: Go **Leaner** Sand, Long straights: Go **Richer** Muddy: Go **Richer**	 Unless very muddy, then go Richer

JETTING CHANGES

Suspension	Front Standard Oil Level	Compression (top) 8 clicks Rebound (bottom) 9 clicks 375 cm	Clockwise/In is **Stiffer**, all components
	Rear Standard	High Speed Damping (hex) Low Speed Damping (screw) Rebound (screw on bottom)	1-1/2 to 2 turns, punch marks aligned 9 clicks, punch marks aligned 5-8 clicks

SUSPENSION CHANGES

SUSPENSION SERVICE

Cheat SheetZ® [generic version to copy]

Oil	Engine	cm no filter	
		cm w/ filter	
	Trans	cm	
Race Sag	mm	Mud: 5/10mm **less sag**	Mud: stiffer on compression/rebound
		Sand: **increase sag** 5/10mm	Sand: stiffer on rebound, **maybe** compression
Plug			
Tires	Front		
	Rear		
Chain		links	
Sprockets		ratio	
Jetting	# MJ	Cold: Go **Richer**	
	# SJ	Very Dry Air: Go **Richer**	
	Clip:	High Humidity/Raining: Go **Leaner**	Unless very muddy, then go Richer
	notch		
		High Altitude: Go **Leaner**	
		Sand, Long straights: Go **Richer**	
		Muddy: Go **Richer**	

JETTING CHANGES

Suspension	Front	Compression (top of forks)	clicks	Clockwise/In is **Stiffer**, all components
	Standard	Rebound (bottom)	clicks	
	Oil Level			
	Rear	High Speed Damping	clicks	Hex nut, punch marks aligned
	Standard	Low Speed Damping	clicks	Screw, punch marks aligned
		Rebound	clicks	Screw on bottom

SUSPENSION CHANGES

SUSPENSION SERVICE

DEALING WITH OLD GAS

Gasoline is what powers our favorite toys but it's also one of the most toxic chemical brews known to mankind. And unlike whiskey or fine wine, it doesn't improve with age. As a matter of fact, today's fuel has essentially zero shelf life and can gum up a carb in as little as two weeks. Here are the do's and don'ts of safely getting rid of the stuff:

- Never, never, never dump gas onto the ground or use it to kill weeds around the house. It makes its way into the underground water supply and brands you as an eco-idiot who thinks that it's okay to poison people.
- Never use gas for cleaning air filters. It dissolves the glue that holds the filter together and there's not a single filter maker that approves of this practice. Use kerosene instead.
- Gas is a carcinogenic, which is Latin for "causes cancer." Keep it off bare skin. Wear nitrile gloves when you handle it.
- Old gas that hasn't yet turned into varnish can be mixed with fresh fuel and used in your lawn mower, truck, snowblower, or car. Pour it through a coffee filter to remove any dirt and then mix it at one gallon old to five gallons new. This is the single best way to dispose of old gas.
- Alternately, take the old gas to a local recycling/hazardous waste facility. Go to www.911earth.com to find the nearest location. Just enter your zip code to find where to go.
- Gas that's too old, too cruddy, or that you don't want to use in your lawn mower can be poured into a metal pan filled with newspaper. The newspaper will soak up the gas and dry out and can be disposed of with regular trash.

This website provides a quick and easy way to find nearby hazardous waste disposal sites. Just enter your zip code.

COPY THAT

Make photocopies of the pages in your owner's manual dealing with suspension adjustment, torque specs, and such. Put those pages in your traveling toolbox to refer to rather than dragging the whole manual along.

for pilot, needle, and main jet. Get some advice from your dealer, local riders, the manual, or purchase a jetting kit (JD or similar) and make the changes.

- Buy at least one new air filter. If the bike only came with one filter, buy two new ones and retire the original. Filters wear out from being repeatedly cleaned.
- Drain and replace all fluids. If the bike has more than 20 hours on it, that includes the suspension components (see Chapter 4). Top off or drain and refill them all depending on age and condition.
- Replace any controls that are worn out or damaged. Typically the clutch lever will be rattling around in its mount. Replace with something better like a Works Connection or ASV pivot lever.
- Add any skid plates or other armor that's needed. A radiator brace won't prevent all damage—nothing will—but it's good, cheap insurance.
- If the hydraulic fluid in the master cylinder is honey-colored or brown, drain the hydraulic lines and replace with the proper grade of fluid. Make sure it's fresh fluid that is just purchased and never opened. Bleed the brakes (see Chapter 3).
- Replace brake pads, front and rear. They've definitely been used.
- Lube all control cables and replace if they're still binding or if they're sticky even after being lubed or have obvious wear.
- Wheel bearings wear out quickly, especially if they are repeatedly attacked by a power washer in the hands of an overzealous owner. With the bike on a stand, spin the wheels to see if they rotate freely or grind to

On four-strokes, that tube running from the head to behind the carb holds expelled oily gunk. Drain it out regularly or you'll be sorry.

Real mud/sand tires are the ticket when things get nasty.

a halt. You can purchase replacement bearing kits from All Balls or PivotWorks that include everything you need and good instructions.

- Wear on suspension parts is harder to evaluate, but if the bike has seen plenty of use, it's safe to assume you need to redo the suspension. One of the good suspension shops can check things out, replace worn parts, and freshen the fluids—all money well spent.
- Repack the silencer. It's guaranteed this is necessary and it actually boosts power.
- Make the bike fit you properly. See Chapter 5.
- Plan on installing new tires, a new chain, and probably sprockets. Factor these costs into your bike-buying budget. Nothing makes a bike seem nicer than fresh meat on the wheels. Chains and sprockets are high-wear items, so as long as you have the rear wheel off, you might as well replace them.

ENDURO, CROSS-COUNTRY, GNCC, AND MUD RACING PREP

When you know you will be racing in the glop, it pays to put some additional prep into your bike. The goal is to make it harder for mud to accumulate and weigh down the bike and easier for you to stay in place and in control. For mud and sand riding, do this:

- Install solid brake rotors to increase brake pad life by as much as 50 percent. With standard slotted rotors, mud gets packed into the slots and grinds the pads down.

Put a couple strips of duct tape over parts of the shroud to keep the mud from sticking.

Looks like fun to us!

Do your first oil change immediately after your break-in ride. With a new thumper, follow that up with a filter change after about an hour or two of riding.

- Spray the underside of fenders, the swingarm, wheels, and front number plate with Pam, Maxima SC1, or WD-40 to make it more difficult for the mud to stick.
- Stick fuel cell/skidplate foam in open areas that collect mud, such as around footpegs, under the carb, etc. Use zip-ties to hold in place as needed. Change the foam between motos. Some aftermarket companies supply kits of precut foam pieces. Acerbis sells a rubber bootie to cover the footpeg pivot so mud can't jam it up. You can also cut up a bicycle tube to do the same thing. Always install the supplied foam if running a skid plate, because otherwise you're creating a mud receptacle.
- Run fork boots or SealSavers in muddy/sandy conditions to protect the fork seals. Mud or sand will wear out seals quickly.
- Make sure handlebar grips are sealed at the bar and safety-wired. If in doubt, apply silicone seal where the grip meets the bar.
- Lube everything, and then lube it again, before you head into the goop. Lube the rims, pivots, plastic, number plates, rubber seals around bearings, levers, etc. Just keep any lube off the seat or you'll be backwards at the first sign of moisture.
- Install a gripper seat. Some are grippier than others.
- Install self-adhesive traction tape (found at any hardware store) to frame points and any plastic where you want to be able to grip the bike with your knees.
- Take apart and waterproof all electrical connections. Take them apart, apply dielectric grease, reassemble, and wrap in vinyl electrical tape.
- Make sure the rear brake pivot is well greased. Take it apart and apply waterproof grease.
- Install grips that have lots of ridges to help your hands hold on.

- Install handguards to block muddy roost ("rooster tails" of mud being flung by the rear wheel of the bike in front of you).
- Sharpen the teeth on the footpegs with a file or Dremel.
- Wear riding gear that keeps you relatively dry, but make sure your gear is vented so you don't overheat—you will be working *hard* out there. Wear gaiters around the top of the boots where they meet your pants or seal with duct tape, as few things are more annoying than riding with a water/mud-filled boot.
- Run mud/sand tires and run the correct low pressure for conditions. See Chapter 3.
- Adjust your jetting to match the weather and humidity. See Chapter 8.
- Run an O- or X-ring sealed chain (there are variations on this) and a steel rear sprocket for longer life and fewer adjustments. Mud and sand wear components out quickly.
- Adjust the race sag and suspension clickers in anticipation of the increased weight. See Chapter 4.

HOW TO BUY A USED BIKE

Do your research first. Unless you know what comparable bikes are selling for in your area—and *only* in your area—you won't know if you're getting a good deal or not. Check out the bikes in the newspaper classifieds, local dealers, at your favorite racetrack, craigslist, eBay, motorcycletrader.com, and any other sources that come to mind. Tell your riding buddies that you're in the market and let them do some of the work for you. Go to www.kbb.com for a Kelly Blue Book guide to

Have cash along so you can put down a deposit if the bike checks out okay.

KEEPING IT YOURS

Theft is a nasty problem in some areas. Try to avoid advertising the fact that your garage holds a bunch of expensive toys. Then be a little paranoid and lock them up while in the garage. Write down your bike's serial numbers and carry the information with you in your wallet so it's on hand if you need to prove a bike is really yours. Buy motorcycle insurance that covers it not only when it's at home, but also when you're riding. Finally, invest in some quick and easy security for the races, such as a cable lock or at least a padlock through a brake disc to keep someone from just rolling it away while you're off at the concession stand.

market value. Give yourself a couple weeks' time to search for a used bike and be prepared to let some deals go by the way—there's always more bikes out there.

When you've found some likely candidates, pay a visit, and be prepared to leave a cash deposit. Check for these clues as to the bike's real condition:

- Is it clean? Really clean, and not just hosed off? Dirt hides problems and a dirty bike means the owner didn't give a damn about maintenance. A lazy owner is going to skip doing the important stuff.
- Look around. Does the seller have good tools, other bikes, or race trophies? Does he sound like someone who knows what he's talking about? Or is he just someone who had enough slack on his credit card to buy a bike and now he's trying to get rid of it? It's usually better to buy from someone who's been riding for a while. Many

newbie owners run their new bikes ragged, never do any maintenance, lose interest as soon as the first mechanical problem surfaces, and then try to dump the bike on an unsuspecting buyer.

- Is it basically stock or heavily modified? Either situation can be a blessing or a curse. A stock bike may need quite a few things to make it competitive and you'll be the one laying out the cash. The flip side is that a heavily modified bike may not be worth what the owner thinks it is and some of the mods may not be good ones, the mods you want, or well executed. By default, any modified or aftermarket part is worth no more—and usually much less—than half what it originally cost (i.e, a $600 pipe is worth no more than $300 to you), so add up the numbers when thinking about whether it's a good buy or not. Many local pro riders sell their modified race or practice bikes at what are often bargain prices considering the modifications. It sounds good, but the catch is that a pro rider usually flogs his bikes, bouncing the motor off the rev limiter, quickly wearing out all those high-buck parts.

- Run your fingers up and down the fork sliders and feel for burrs, nicks, or suspension fluid from blown seals. It's not a deal-breaker but is one more thing to negotiate with the seller.
- Is anything repainted? Assume that the paint is covering up heavy wear or a problem.
- Squat down behind the bike and look at the pegs. They should be pointing slightly upward or at least level. If they're sagging, the bike has led a hard life and has been pounded to bits.
- A bike that has seen a lot of use in mud will have very dull aluminum, worn bearings, worn chain, faded/scratched plastic and graphics, seized fasteners, and is likely to have other problems that will increase your out-of-pocket expense to fix.
- Don't be misled by new cosmetics, graphics, or plastic. Those are good signs but can also mean the seller is trying to distract you from less obvious mechanical problems.
- Always assume you're going to be spending money on something, whether it's a top-end job, repairs, new tires, chain, or whatever. Add these expenses to your list. (You are keeping a list, aren't you?) Assume that everything is going to cost more than you think. A set of tires alone is about $120. A chain will be $60 to $80. The total gets big quickly. Take notes, add it up, and when you're ready to talk price, point out what it's going to cost you to fix things.
- Feel the pipe and cylinder. Are they hot? Maybe the owner started the bike in order to make sure it *would* start when you showed up? Let it cool off by asking a lot of questions, then let him start it up for you. Watch what he does as some bikes have a routine you need to follow.
- Look for smoke. White smoke at start-up is usually just condensation being burnt off, but if it never goes away it may be a coolant leak. Dark, oily smoke after the bike has warmed up is never a good sign, even from a two-stroke engine.
- Look underneath the bike for damage, leaks, and so on. Bring along a bright flashlight and use it to carefully look over things. A favorite seller's trick is to have the bike in a dimly-lit garage at night.
- With the bike on a stand, wiggle the forks, bars, and swingarm to look for excessive play, grinding noises, or binding. Spin the wheels and apply the brakes. Take a close look at both sprockets and check how much adjustment room is left on the chain adjusters.
- Take your time. If the seller wants you to decide quickly and pay up because he has some pressing appointment, that's a warning sign to head elsewhere.
- Ride the bike if possible, run it through all the gears, and listen for anything that sounds or feels wrong. Ideally,

bring along an experienced friend, preferably someone who owns the same or similar model who will recognize problems. You may be too overwhelmed by the thrill of a new bike and miss the obvious.

- Pull the seat and see if the air filter is clean and fresh or dirty and torn. If it is dirty and torn, you probably don't want the bike no matter what.
- Do your math: (1) What you want to pay, (2) minus what it's going to cost you to fix any problems, and (3) start your negotiating by politely listing the negatives you see or parts that need replacement and what those will cost you to fix.
- It's best to wait for the seller to name his price and then counter with what you're willing to pay. If he keeps asking you to name a price, ask him: "What's your absolute rock-bottom low cash price you'll take today?" Keep talking and you'll probably have a deal. Having cash on hand is always a deal closer, but don't advertise the fact that you're bringing it along until you feel comfortable mentioning it. If you've done your research, you'll know more about what the bike is worth locally than the seller does.
- A few words of warning: If you get bad vibes from talking to the seller—any negatives at all that get your inner radar perking—trust your gut and walk away from the deal. Dirt bikes are a favorite target of thieves because they're seldom titled and easy to resell. Never meet a seller by yourself in some secluded spot. And if you're the seller, always have someone else at home with you.
- Ask the seller for documentation that proves he's the owner.
- Got a deal? A bill of sale, signed and dated with the amount paid is the minimum information you want as a record of the sale. Also write down the seller's address, driver's license number, full name, and other details.

Chapter 3
Wheels, Brakes, and Tires

Going fast isn't just about the motor or your right wrist. While tires, wheels, and brakes aren't the sexy choices for where to spend your time and money, their importance is proven by the factory pros, who get fresh tires before the start of every moto. Fortunately for all of us Average Joes who have to pay for our own toys, the necessary skills to take care of these items fall into that "anybody can do it" category. Here's what you need to know.

GIMME A BRAKE
Make sure your brakes can haul you down from insane speeds. Start with the brake pads:

- If it's a brand new bike, before your first ride, spray contact cleaner on the rotors and wipe them clean with a towel. The factories coat the rotors with an anti-corrosion treatment that, if not removed, ends up on your brake pads and reduces their effectiveness.

- Inspect the pads regularly and replace them often—at least a couple times each season for an active racer. Pads get less effective as they wear and grime gets burnt into their surface. The smart approach is to replace pads every few tire changes since the wheels are already off.

- Dirty or greasy pad? If you can't replace them immediately, take the pads off and rub them over a sheet of emery paper in a figure-eight pattern. Pads that are worn or grimy won't do the job.

- Get the right pads. Pad construction is based on intended use. Get OEM or look for the words "semi-metallic" or "sintered metal" on the package for most conditions.

- To replace the pads, remove the cap over the threaded brake pin and unthread the pin using an Allen wrench. Clean off any corrosion on the pin, add a layer of anti-seize, and put it aside.

- Slide off the backing plates and the pads. Note how things go together.

The difference between new and used pads is graphic. Pads shrink and become glazed with use. New ones are what you need.

- Spray some silicone lube on the pistons to clear out any grime and make them slide easier.
- Put the new pads with backing plates salvaged from the old pads back into the brake housing. You may have to push the piston into the caliper to provide room for the new, thicker pads.
- Make sure you have clean, fresh brake fluid in the system. See the next section.
- Seat your brakes as described next.

Seat Your Brakes

New brake pads need to adjust to their new home. After installing new brake pads, the first time you go riding, do this:

- First, clean off the discs with contact cleaner and a clean towel to remove any dirt or protective coating.
- Ride on flat ground and slam the brakes on hard. Pay attention while doing this and don't be a dork and crash.
- Repeat the hard braking routine a half-dozen times and you're good to go.

Let It Bleed

If the brake fluid looks clean (clear, not honey-colored) and is at the "full" mark on the reservoir but the brake still feels spongy, then you have air trapped in the system. It's time to bleed the brakes.

- There are various brake bleeding kits and special fittings that simplify the job, but you really don't need more than an empty water bottle, some clear tubing, a third hand or a helper, and an 8mm wrench.

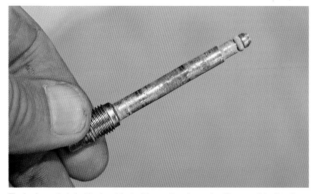

The brake pad pin holder is subjected to nonstop abuse. Any time you take it out, clean it off and put anti-seize lube on the threads before reinstalling.

If the view in your master cylinder shows brownish brake fluid, you're due for new fluid.

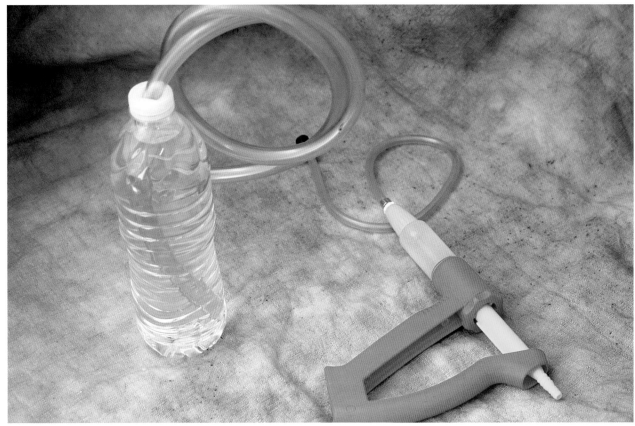

You can buy professional brake bleeding systems such as the Motion Pro unit on the right or make your own with some tubing and an empty water bottle.

Wrap a rag around the reservoir to catch overflow or drips. Brake fluid eats through paint.

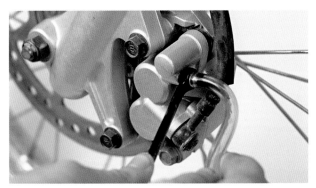

A helper makes bleeding the brakes easier.

• Remove the master cylinder cover, being careful not to let any dirt fall in. Tuck a clean rag around the reservoir to catch any drips because brake fluid damages paint and plastic.

• If the old brake fluid is goopy looking, use a rag or kitchen baster to suck it out of the reservoir, rather than pumping the crud through the lines. If the old brake fluid is yellow or brown, it's junk and you need to completely flush it out.

• Use the correct brake fluid as listed in your owner's manual. Use a brand new never-opened container. Brake fluid is a humectant (absorbs moisture), and moisture is one thing you don't want in your brake lines.

• Pull the brake lever and loosen the 8mm bleeder bolt on the caliper slightly. Old fluid and air bubbles will come out into the tubing and into the bottle. Tighten the bleeder bolt again, add more fresh fluid, and repeat the process until there's only clean new fluid coming out and no more air bubbles. Doing all of this is quicker if you have a helper.

• If you're doing everything right, you will be refilling the reservoir three or four times total. Keep at it until the spongy feeling is gone and no more air bubbles or old brake fluid are visible.

- When replacing brake lines or if dealing with a really stubborn case, unbolt the caliper so it hangs free and the brake lines are as close to vertical and straight as you can manage.
- The factories usually ship their dirt bikes with DOT 3 brake fluid, which is adequate but not the best for hardcore racing. When replacing the original brake fluid, drain all of it out and switch to a racing DOT 3, 4, or 5.1 (not DOT 5 which is for Harleys) that has a high dry boiling point designation. Use name brand (BelRay, Motul, etc.) motorcycle-specific products, not the cheapo stuff from the auto parts store.
- After the system is bled, some pro mechanics use a zip-tie to hold the brake lever on and leave it overnight to let any remaining air bubbles work their way to the top. This also tests the system to be sure there are no leaks.

More Pucker Power

No lectures here about stopping fast. We all want great brakes that haul us down from insane speeds with no drama. Everything else being equal, it's the rider who can brake harder that's going to win the race into and out of the corners. Learning how to brake hard is the topic of another book, but having the equipment to out-stop your competition is something anybody can tackle. Here's what you need to do:

- Set the controls so you can get to them quickly and confidently. If your rear brake lever is tucked in too close to the frame, bend it out or buy an after-market unit. Position the front lever to where it's most naturally at hand.
- This is technique, but it bears repeating: USE THE FRONT BRAKE! The bulk of your machine's braking power is at the front wheel, not the back.
- Keep fresh pads and fresh brake fluid with a high temperature threshold on the bike. This is a no-brainer.
- Fresh tires let you brake harder. 'Nuff said.
- Swap out the stock brake hoses for stiffer, larger-diameter, stainless-steel aftermarket units. Be sure to use the supplied new crush washers. Crush washers are for one-time use.
- Replace the stock brake rotor with an oversize unit. More disc surface area means more braking power. Oversize rotors cost about $200 to $400 and come with a different mounting bracket that relocates the caliper. An oversize disc combined with stainless-steel brake lines delivers running-into-a-wall stopping power.
- Off-road and XC racers who spend a lot of time in the mud should switch to a solid brake disc because it does a better job of keeping the brake pads alive through a long, muddy day.

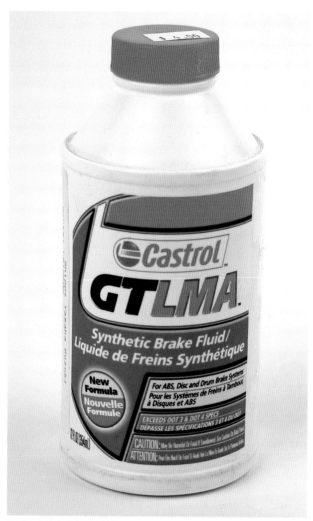

Buy the right stuff. Get the high-temperature "racing" brake fluid. Buy a fresh can and keep it capped.

BIGGER IS BETTER: OVERSIZE BRAKES

When it comes to bang for buck and ease of installation, this modification is well worth it. Expect to pay in the area of $200 to $350 for the oversize brake kit disc, pads, and the new bracket to relocate the caliper. This is also a good time to install stainless-steel brake lines. What you need to know:

- Only replace the front disc. Rears don't need to be bigger and most of your braking power is in the front brake, not the rear. Big bikes benefit more from an oversize disc than a 250F or 125 smoker.
- Take off the front wheel, the stock disc, and unbolt the caliper from the fork leg.
- Install the oversize disc after first checking whether it's facing the right way or not (check the instructions). If you've already replaced the front disc a couple of times, or even if not, it might be smart to use new bolts and thread-lock if called for. Torque to specs.

- Install the aftermarket bracket to the caliper and fork leg. It will use some parts from the stock unit. Torque to specs.
- Install new brake pads (most kits come with them; if not, buy some). You don't want to mix a new disc with an old set of pads because the surfaces won't mate well, making the whole project pointless.
- Remount the wheel, squeeze the brakes a few times, and make sure everything is working properly.
- Clean off the new disc with contact cleaner and a clean towel.
- Break in the new pads and disc by riding at slow to moderate speeds in the pit area (not the track), applying the brakes to heat them up, and coasting in between to let them cool off. Repeat this heat-up cycle a half-dozen times. This also seats the new brake pads.
- Now hit the track, but be careful at first. Take some time to learn how these new brakes respond. Some brands are more sudden than others, and in all cases, the increase in whoa-power is large. Respect it.

STAINLESS-STEEL LINES

The OEM stock brake lines are rubber and fabric and relatively soft. Stainless-steel lines don't flex and provide a better feel at the lever. Installation is simple, although it can be a bit messy. Here's the drill:

- Remove the reservoir caps and soak up the brake fluid with rags, paper towels, or a kitchen baster.
- Unbolt the brake line from the caliper and let it drain. Then unbolt it from the reservoir and remove.
- The stainless-steel line(s) will come with new crush washers and these must be torqued to specs, so check your shop manual for the number. Crush washers are one-time use, but if you mess it up, you can find replacements at the auto parts store.
- Pour fresh brake fluid into the reservoir and if you have one, use one of the brake-bleeding suction tools to draw fluid into the line.
- Do the brake-bleeding routine until you're sure the lines are purged of trapped air.
- Check for leaks and clean up any spilled brake fluid.

BRAKE AND WHEEL TIPS

Here's some basic stuff to remember:

Axles Don't Need Grease

Any time you remove an axle, clean it thoroughly and buff off corrosion or burrs. Axles don't rotate and don't need grease—the bearings are what rotate. Putting grease on an axle just makes it gum up. Hit the axle with some spray-on lube as corrosion protection before reinstalling.

A larger front disc lets you hit the turns deeper and harder than the other guy. It's a very useful performance mod.

Add stainless-steel brake lines to complete the switch to a larger front disc. Stainless-steel brake lines improve feel at the lever and overall braking action. Not bad for $50 to $75 per line.

When you pull the axle for a tire change, stick it in the end of the muffler to keep it clean and at-hand.

Disc Pad Mod

Sometimes the hardest part of a tire change is sliding the brake disc back between the pads while you're trying to balance a rear wheel, the axle, and a bunch of spacers all at the same time. Try this: Take a file or grinder to the edge of the back of the pads and chamfer them so they're curved rather than straight. This will let the brake disc slide right between the pads without a fight and won't affect the braking.

Keep the Axle at Hand

When pulling an axle, keep it out of the dirt by sliding it into the open end of your muffler. It'll usually fit, and this keeps it handy and clean until time to reinstall.

WHEEL OF FORTUNE

Changing a tire when it's sitting on the ground is zero fun. If you can't afford a tire-changing stand, go looking for an old 15- or 16-inch car rim (sans tire). You can usually find these for free at junk yards, garage sales, by the side of the road, or waiting at the curb for trash day. Put your wheel on the car rim, rotor side down to protect it. Just raising the tire off the ground these few inches will make your tire changes quicker and easier.

CHANGING TIRES AND TUBES THE RIGHT WAY

There aren't very many riders who enjoy changing tires. Even when you know what you're doing and have all the right tools, it can still be a battle sometimes. Still, putting new rubber on your bike and fixing flats is a necessary evil, and learning how to do it properly and quickly is an art you must master because you are going to need fresh meat to go fast.

There have been at least one million magazine articles written about how to change a tire and tube so we're not going to repeat that here. The magazines run these stories every couple issues, so pick up a copy.

Instead, here are tips and key steps for changing tires or tubes in three situations: at home, at the track, and out on the trail.

Home Sweet Home

There's no place like the comforts of home when tackling a tire change or flat fix. Here's how to make it even easier.

- Have the tools. It's an investment you won't regret. A tire-changing stand (good ones start at around $100), a set of spoon-type irons, valve core remover, wrench for the rim lock, and an air compressor or tire pump. Optional tools are a Bead Buddy, Bead Popper, and valve stem puller.
- Supplies on hand: spare or new tube, talcum powder (the real stuff that has talcum as the main ingredient), and some glass cleaner or dishwasher soap.
- Putting on a new tire? Warm it up either outside in the sun or inside the house. Warm tires go on easier.
- Don't back the rim lock nut completely off. Loosen until the nut is right at the end. When both beads are broken, tap the rim lock in to loosen it.
- Keep your tire irons relatively close together as you work around the tire. Most people space them too far apart and try to muscle the tire off—that's wrong.
- Start with the tire irons between the valve and the rim lock.
- With the old tire off, sprinkle talcum powder into the new tire to keep the new tube from chafing.
- Very lightly inflate the tube and insert it into the tire. Apply soapy water to the tire bead.
- Now insert the valve stem through the opening on the rim and lightly secure it with a nut. With the tube in the tire, work the tire onto the rim with first your hands and body weight, then using the tire irons, taking small bites—6 inches or less between the tire irons.
- Some brands of tires have a small paint mark on the sidewall. That's the lightest point of the tire and where your tire valve should go.
- Lift the bead of the tire with two irons high enough to push the rim lock up to clear the bead of the tire.
- Flip the tire, apply some more soapy water to the bead, and lever the tire onto the rim. Push down on the tire as you work to keep it off the bead.
- Done properly, the last few inches of the tire will require only a moderate amount of effort to pry over the rim.

WHY YOU NEED FOUR WHEELS FOR YOUR MOTORCYCLE

One of the best investments you can make is a second set of wheels. Having a second set allows you to go to the races with fresh rubber ready to go for the actual races, while using worn tires for practice. It's a good feeling to go to the start line with fresh meat on your rims. A second set of wheels also allows you to bring along a set of specialty tires—mud or sand tires, for example—to deal with unexpected conditions. And of course a spare set of wheels means that a flat tire isn't a day-ender.

You can buy used wheel sets on eBay or craigslist or get new ones laced up just the way you want them so you'll know they'll have good bearings and aren't dinged. Warp Racing (www.warp9racing.com) is a good place to shop because their wheels come with brake discs and sprocket already installed. You can quickly swap out the stockers and slide in the Warp Wheels in a matter of minutes because all the hardware is already attached.

Make tire changes simpler by having multiple tire spoons (one of them big and long for the added leverage), a Motion Pro Bead Popper (the chisel-like blue thing), and a Bead Buddy. Talcum powder—the real stuff—and soapy water are also necessities. The tire wrench at the bottom has one end with a wrench to fit the axle nut, which comes in damn handy out on the trail and far from the truck.

Sprinkle baby powder (the good stuff with talcum powder) inside the tire to reduce friction between the tube and tire.

Don't go all King Kong on the rim lock. It only needs to be snug, not super-tight. If it's too tight, it will cause problems.

This is what happens if you tighten the nut on the valve stem and the tube starts to spin inside the tire—it tears the valve stem completely off the tire, giving you an unfixable flat.

Some tire brands have a small paint mark on the sidewall indicating the lightest spot on the tire. The tire valve should go here when installing the tire.

- Reinflate the tire and check that it's seated properly (sometimes bouncing the wheel on the floor a few times helps).
- If there are any air bubbles showing on the rim, you pinched the tube and get to start over.
- Tighten the rim lock but don't crank it down like you're King Kong. Actual torque specs for a rim lock are around 9 foot-pounds—that's not a lot.

At the Races

A lot of riders choose to—or have to—change tires or tubes at the races. If this is the case, usually you're short on time, short of tools, and not in the best mood. Flat tires can do that to you. Here's how to make it go down easier:

- Delegate: If there's a trackside vendor with a tire-changing machine, it's worth it to pay them to do the work for you. You'll have more time to ride, less chance of suffering a pinched tube, and won't wear yourself out wrestling with stubborn rubber.
- If the problem is a flat, try one of the aerosol tire sealants/ inflators. Sometimes you'll get lucky and they'll do the trick, at least long enough to get your moto done. Replace your can of tire sealant once a year, as they eventually become stale and useless.
- You can't fix a flat without a replacement tube, so pack along a spare—both sizes if you have the room, but if not, a 21-inch front tube can be used in either wheel, but not the other way around.

- Gotta do it yourself? First get a static stand for the wheel. A trash can, your truck bed, or at least placing a sheet of cardboard or rags on the ground to protect the bearings is enough.
- Remember: Warm rubber installs easier than cold. If it's a bright sunny day, leave the new tire out in the sun.
- Remove the valve core, loosen the rim lock, and then kneel on the tire to break the bead. If you've had a flat, it may already be off the bead.
- If you're working on the ground, you have less leverage, so use your body to make up for it. Use your knees and feet to break the bead and get leverage on the tire irons.
- Lubricate the bead. If you don't have any soap available, try some WD-40 or water to help get a stubborn tire bead in place.
- The actual tire and tube change process is no different than doing it at home.

Warm rubber installs easier than cold, hard rubber. Let it soak up the rays first.

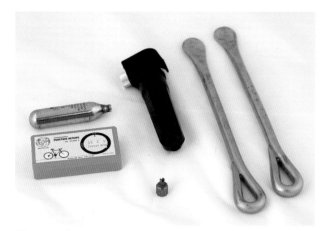

What you need in your trail-riding fanny pack: zip-ties, small tire irons, CO_2 inflater, wrenches to fit the axle and rim lock, and a patch kit or spare tube.

You can reuse a tube unless it starts to look like this, with obvious wear, the writing on the tube worn off, and a rusted valve stem.

Add some color to your wheels. A colored valve cap makes the tire valve easier to find. A billet rim lock covers the rim lock threads so they don't corrode, which would slow down a tire change.

On the Trail

Fixing a flat on the trail assumes you have a spare tube or a patch kit and a way to inflate the tire, plus a few tools in your fanny pack to do the work.

- On at least one wheel, have a valve cap that includes a built-in valve core remover.
- Invest in some wheel spacers—our favorites are Zip-Ty Racing—that stay in place when the wheel is removed. It speeds up tire changes and is one less thing to get lost.
- Got a flat and no spare tube or a patch kit? Use some zip-ties or wire from a fence to secure a flat tire to the rim and slowly make your way back to the truck.
- Find something to prop the bike up, preferably with the wheel off the ground. If there's nothing at hand, lay the bike on the ground.
- Once the wheel is off, remove the valve core and loosen the rim lock.
- Find something to put on the ground underneath the wheel to keep dirt out of the bearings. Dry brush, your gloves or jacket—whatever is at hand.
- You already know the drill from here: break the bead (use two tire irons or stand on the tire), pull the tube, fix or replace it, reinstall, and reinflate.

Valve Nuts No-No

Even with good rim locks, tires and tubes can spin on the rim under braking and acceleration. If they spin too far, they can rip the valve right out of the tube. That's why you don't tighten the valve nut down against the rim. You want to allow for the tube to spin a little if it comes to that. Hondas have avoided this problem for many years by using slightly oversized valve stem holes in the rim and a rubber boot instead of a nut.

Twisted Valve Stem

If you notice that the valve stem has tipped to an angle, it's spun inside the rim and may be a prelude to a flat. Deflate the tire completely by removing the valve core, loosen the rim lock, and turn the tire to straighten the valve stem. Some soapy water on the bead will help the tire move if it's stubborn.

Add Some Color

Switch from the basic black valve stem caps to something colorful. This is a visual reminder to check tire pressure by making the valve easy to find. Billet covers for the rim lock are also a good thing and aren't just for looks as they protect the rim lock threads from corroding and being hard to remove.

TIRE NUMBERS

There are a lot of markings and numbers on a tire, but you only care about three numbers and one mark (a directional arrow, if present). Here's the code for the numbers:

- The first number is the width of the tire in millimeters.
- The second number is the height of the tire as a percentage of its width, otherwise known as the "aspect ratio."
- The third number is the rim diameter it fits.

Now comes the gotcha in all this: The tire manufacturers don't measure their products in the same way, so never assume that just because the numbers match, that competing brands are indeed exactly the same. Some will be a little taller or a little wider than tires with comparable numbers. However, all of the tire sizes of any one company should match the numbers, so a 120 tire should be wider than the same company's 110 model.

Tire Size Conversion Chart

Since the USA is the only non-metric modern nation, if you're still thinking in "inches" you will be confused by tire size numbers when you go shopping. Adding to the confusion is that tire measurements have changed over the years, resulting in an "Old Metric" size and a "New Metric" size, which is what you'll now see marked on the tires. Here's a conversion chart:

Front Tires

New Metric	Old Metric	Inch
60/100	90/80	2.50 to 2.75
70/100	90/80	2.75 to 3.00
80/100	100/800	3.00 to 3.25

Rear Tires

New Metric	Old Metric	Inch
80/100	80/90	2.50 to 3.60
90/100	110/90	3.60 to 4.10
100/100	120/80	4.00 to 4.10
110/100	130/80	4.00 to 4.50
120/100	140/80	5.00 to 5.10

EVERYTHING YOU NEED TO KNOW ABOUT TIRE PRESSURE

Besides having good tires with adequate meat on them, you need to understand the role of air pressure and how to manage it. Here's the scoop:

- Get a good, accurate tire gauge; not those stick things. Spend the money because you need to be able to accurately and consistently measure tire pressure.

- The ballpark tire pressure you want in most average conditions is 12–13 front and 12 rear. This is operating temperature, not the cold tire setting. Your tires heat up within just a lap or two.
- Tire pressure changes with air temperature, ground temperature, riding time, and track conditions. Your tires start heating up and pressure rises as soon as you start riding.
- Check tire pressure just before heading out for practice and just before you line up for each moto. Factor in that the tires will heat up and pressure will increase.
- Rear tires heat up faster and tire pressure can increase by as much as 6 psi after only a few laps.
- Front tires also heat up, but the increase is more gradual (smaller air volume, smaller contact patch, less friction since it's not driven).
- A hard, blue-groove track will increase tire pressure buildup faster than a soft track.
- If your front tire won't stick in turns and deflects on bumps easily, it has too much air.
- If your front tire won't stick in corners and wallows around like a pregnant hippo, it doesn't have enough air.
- If you're riding in deep mud or deep sand, lower rear tire pressure to 8 to 10 psi unless the mud has so much bite or is so sticky that the front end won't stay down. In that case, increase rear tire pressure so it spins easier and cleans out.
- Rocky tracks require higher tire pressure. Think 15–14 front and 12–13 rear.
- The harder and drier the track, the more air pressure you need at each end and the softer the tire. Hardpack tires are actually quite soft, but the increased friction means that the tires heat up quicker.
- Sand/mud tires—the ones designed for "soft" conditions—are actually the stiffest of any off-road tire in order to reach down into the dirt and mud and grab some traction.
- The smaller the bike, the higher the tire pressure. Since they have less power, 50cc minis should be running 20psi; 60–80cc bikes should be 14 to 18 psi.
- Nitrogen is much slower to heat up and can be used instead of plain old air. It's what the pro mechanics use to keep tire pressure consistent. You can buy nitrogen at some gas stations and welding supply centers.
- The stock tubes that come with the bike are typically low-cost items—one of the little things the factory accountants figure we won't notice—so plan on installing a new and better one soon after you buy your new bike.
- Limit the chances of flats by buying good, heavy-duty tubes. This isn't some place where you want to save a few bucks. A thin, light-duty tube saves some unsprung weight but is more likely to puncture.
- Match the tube size to the tire. Using a 110-size tube in a 100 tire will make it more likely to be pinched; conversely a tube that's smaller than the tire will have to be inflated more to make up the size difference.

Use a good tire gauge designed for low pressure readings.

There will be days when no matter what you do, you can't break the bead loose from the rim. A Motion Pro Bead Popper will be your lifesaver and won't damage the rim or tire.

A valve puller makes getting the tube's valve stem properly inserted about a thousand times easier than the usual pinched fingers method.

BEAD POPPER

There will come a day in your tire-changing life when you find yourself in a bloody-knuckled battle with a tire that simply won't break its seal with the rim. Even the usual trick of standing on the tire is to no avail. Dynamite would work, but it's too messy. The solution is a Bead Popper from Motion Pro. Used with a dead-blow hammer, this wedge is just the right angle and size to drive through the bead seal and let you get on with the rest of the tire change. It costs about $12 and if you only need to use it once a year, it will more than pay for itself in reduced misery.

THE VALVE PULLER

Instead of trying to wiggle the tire stem through the hole in the rim, use a valve puller. One end threads into the valve stem and you pull on the handle to guide it into place. It saves you skinned knuckles, mucho frustration, and a lot of time. Get one for about $10 to $15 from DRC/Dirt Freak.

TRUING YOUR WHEELS

Tightening spokes is one of those dirt bike maintenance routines that shouldn't be skipped, especially with a new bike. Spokes need to bed in and will loosen over time, especially near the rim lock(s). Here's how to check and adjust your spokes:

- With the bike on a stand, spin the wheel and look for wobbles as it spins. A wobbling wheel means either loose spokes or a dinged rim.

The ultimate spoke wrench is a spoke torque wrench like this Fasst Company version. Not cheap, but the best way to be sure spokes are evenly tightened and wheels straight.

- While spinning the wheel slowly, feel for loose spokes. If you can waggle it back and forth, it's loose.
- With a proper size spoke wrench, start adjusting the spoke tension in small increments, doing every third spoke.
- Work around the wheel several times, tightening only a small amount each time, as otherwise you'll pull the wheel out of shape.
- It's inaccurate, but everybody does it: the "ping" test. Bounce the spoke wrench off each spoke. A loose spoke will sound dull, flat, and low pitched; one that's properly adjusted will ping cleanly; too-tight spokes will sound sharp and high-pitched.
- If you have a lot of loose spokes on one side, remember that you also need to adjust the ones on the opposite side of the wheel to equalize the tension. You need to both tighten and loosen spokes on both sides of the wheel to get rid of a wobble.
- If your wheel is seriously out of round, consider taking it to a specialist, either a shop that builds wheels or a bicycle shop. Truing a wheel that's seriously out of round is something of an art and requires patience and practice plus a truing stand.
- Don't over-tighten spokes. A tight spoke is more likely to break and it allows nearby spokes to loosen.
- Your goal is to have a wobble-free wheel where each spoke is equally tensioned.

PULSING BRAKES

If you can feel your front brake lever surging back and forth as you ride, you have a warped brake rotor. You can maybe fix a tweaked disc by following the steps below, but if not, then you'll have to replace the rotor. Try this first:

- Spread the caliper open by pushing it toward the disc so the piston retracts. This gives you a reference point when checking the disc.
- Align the caliper so you can see daylight between the disc and pads on both sides.
- Rotate the wheel slowly, watching the disc. The warped portion will lean toward one of the pads.
- Stop the wheel and use a Sharpie to mark the point where it contacts the pad. Repeat several times so you're sure you have the warped area(s) identified.
- Use a large adjustable wrench to gently bend the disc in the opposite direction of the warp. Take it easy; don't show off your He-man strength. Spin the wheel and check your progress.
- Keep at it until the warp is gone or you realize it's hopeless and time to order a new disc.

Center the disc in the caliper. Spin it and watch it as it passes between the pads.

Chapter 4
Life's Ups and Downs: Dealing with Your Suspension

Most people think it's the motor that determines how fast you can go, but it's actually the suspension that has the final say in the matter. If you can't keep the wheels on the ground and driving, it doesn't matter how much horsepower the engine is spewing out.

Suspension tuning is both an art and a science to the point where many riders are afraid to do anything. That's too bad because the truth is it's simple to become a wizard at suspension setup. The next few pages will show you what you need to know.

When there are big problems with your suspension or it's time for a rebuild, unless you've got the time and tools to tackle it, you're almost always better off letting a suspension specialist shop do the work for you. They've got the tools, expertise, and patience to do it properly.

SUSPENSION TUNING SIMPLIFIED

Suspension tuning in two words: *Do something*. When your suspension isn't acting the way you think it should, make some changes. If it gets worse, you've learned you need to

go the opposite direction. If it gets better, keep adjusting it until it gets worse, then back it off. Your owner's manual is your reference point in all this, but even if you left it at home you can still follow this advice. It's almost always better to do something than to just slow down because you're afraid to mess with the suspension. Do something!

CRAM COURSE: HOW TO BECOME A SUSPENSION WIZARD

Be the envy of your racing buddies—or just a lot faster than they are—by becoming a suspension wizard. Here's how:

- Always have your shock linkage, swingarm pivot, and steering head properly greased up and working properly. The more often you use power washers, the more often you need to grease things up.
- Learn how to properly set the sag and do it as conditions require.
- Learn what each of the clickers do and how to use them to tune your suspension.
- Learn to interpret what the bike is telling you in how it reacts to the track.
- Suspension only moves down (compression) and up (rebound). You work with separate adjusters to control these two movements.
- Test your suspension in order to set it up properly by knowing which track features affect which part of the suspension package.
- Send out your suspension to the pro shops who know what they're doing and have the tools to do it right and quickly. Have them revalve to your riding (dressed) weight and real-world riding ability.
- Have the pro shops change the fluids in the suspension about every 20 to 30 hours of riding time. Most guys run their suspensions for too long so the fluids are about as useful as maple syrup.

SETTING SAG

There are two types of sag: static (also called free) sag and rider (also called race) sag. Setting sag is the single most important part of suspension tuning because of its effect on total suspension behavior. Get this wrong or ignore it and all bets are off.

Rider (Race) Sag

- With the bike on a stand and the wheels off the ground, measure from the left inside fender bolt to a point on the rear axle. Use a sag-setting tool or use a metric tape measure. Write this measurement down.
- Put the bike on the ground and the rider dressed in all his gear on the bike. Bounce up and down on the suspension and then sit where you'd normally sit on the bike. Ideally, have someone hold the bike so the rider's entire weight is on the machine. Do not stand up. Have someone repeat the measurement between those two points. Write it down.

Do something! There's no reason to be afraid of your suspension. Becoming a suspension wizard means learning a few simple procedures, a few terms, and a willingness to experiment with clicker settings.

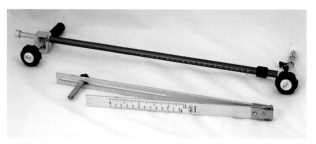

A Motion Pro sag tool (the blue one on top) lets you set the sag solo. Convenient if there's no one around. The folding sag tool will easily fit into most toolboxes.

- The desired rider (race) sag depends on bike size and manufacturer recommendation. You need to know what the recommended race sag is from the manufacturer or the suspension shop.
- Subtract the second measurement from the first. If the answer is either more or less than the recommended race sag, you need to adjust the spring preload by turning the preload adjuster.
- Turning the preload adjuster clockwise decreases rider sag.
- Turning it counterclockwise increases rider sag.
- Note that you only have to loosen the lock nut; you can then turn the preload adjuster with your hands if there's room.
- Pay attention to where you start turning the adjustment ring or use a marker to provide a reference point. On average, each turn of the shock preload ring is equal to about 3 to 5mm of sag; so counting turns is the quick way to get the number you want.
- Have the rider sit on the machine again and repeat the measurements.
- Repeat the adjustments on the preload adjuster until you get the desired race sag setting, then tighten the locking ring with a drift and hammer or locking screw (KTMs).

All you need to set sag is a helper and a measuring tape—preferably metric—or a sag-setting tool such as this metal Race Tools unit.

A pushbutton is much simpler than digging around with a screwdriver or risking the loss of the tiny stock screws. The pushbuttons install in minutes.

Static (Free) Sag

- Static sag can only be checked after rider sag has been set. Static sag is how much the bike sags under its own weight.
- With the bike off the stand and no rider, push down on the back end a few times and let the suspension settle. Repeat the earlier measurements and write it down.
- Generally you want to see between 25 and 45mm of free sag. If it doesn't fall within this range, a spring change is needed.
- Less than 25mm free sag indicates a stiffer spring is needed.
- More than 35mm calls for a softer spring.
- For those of you not yet metric-minded, 25mm = 1 inch (actually 25.4mm).

THE (IMPORTANT) LITTLE THINGS YOU PROBABLY FORGOT

Before blaming the suspension for some problem, be sure you've paid attention to these things:

- If you're getting head shake, are you sure the steering head bearing is tight enough? If the front end flops side to side with no resistance, it's too loose. It should require just a light push to move; it shouldn't be swinging in the breeze like a weather vane.
- Is tire pressure correct? A flat tire or one that's over-inflated will destroy the handling.
- Did you bleed the air out of the forks? Forks build up air pressure as you ride and that pressure needs to be released. Put the bike on a stand so the forks are off the ground and be sure to wait until the bike has cooled off before taking out the screw or pushing the release button.

SHOCK WIZARDRY

A modern dirt bike's shock has four possible adjustments:

1. Spring preload
2. Rebound
3. Low-speed compression
4. High-speed compression

The following sections explain how to master each of them:

Note: All shocks are not alike. Refer to your manual to make sure adjustments are in the correct direction for your model.

1. Spring Preload

Spring preload is how you adjust the free sag and rider sag. By turning the adjustment ring on the shock, you compress or lengthen (or soften or harden, if it's easier to think of it that way) the shock spring.

- Once you loosen the locking collar with a drift and hammer, you can do the rest of it by hand if there's room. There's no need to continue to use the drift and hammer.
- Adjusting preload does not make the bike taller or shorter.
- Spray some lube on the threads so the locking collar and adjuster are easy to rotate.

- Depending on the bike, each full revolution of the adjusting ring will adjust the sag from 1 to 4mm—your manual should have the exact number. If the adjusting ring doesn't have a painted reference mark, add one with a Sharpie.
- See the earlier section on free sag to figure out whether your spring rate is correct.

2. Rebound

Rebound is your control switch over how fast the shock returns to fully extended after hitting a bump or landing a jump. If it rebounds too fast, the rear end will be too busy and may even pitch you off. If it rebounds too slowly, it won't be ready for the next bump. What you need to know:

- Your manual will pinpoint the location of the rebound damping adjuster. It is typically at the bottom of the shock where the linkage arms are located.
- Find the reference mark when you make your adjustments.
- Turning the rebound screw clockwise (IN) slows down the rebound (check your manual to be sure, though!).
- Turning the rebound screw counterclockwise (OUT) speeds up the rebound.
- If the rear end is kicking straight up over square-edged bumps, the rebound is too fast. Turn the rebound screw IN.
- If the rear end noticeably kicks up, turn the rebound screw IN.
- If the rear end feels like it's falling down into the bump and doesn't want to come up, the rebound is too slow. Turn the rebound screw OUT.
- If the shock rebound is too slow, the bike will consistently jump front end high.
- Check your manual for how many clicks are available and how many clicks from a full turn—it's usually four clicks for a full turn of the adjuster. Turn it all the way in, then start counting the clicks out.

A factory shock is a piece of unobtainium that gives the lucky factory pro an unmatched ride. But even if you could get one of these shocks, if you don't know how to tune it, you wouldn't see any benefit.

The shock rebound adjuster is usually at the lower end of the shock, often hiding behind the linkage arms. Sometimes to get access you'll need another rider to lift up or compress the suspension so you can get at it.

Get comfortable with the spring preload adjuster on your shock. You'll be using it often.

The low-speed compression (LSC) adjuster is the screw slot inside the larger nut on your shock reservoir. The hex-head nut is the high-speed compression (HSC) adjuster. You'll spend the most time with the low-speed adjuster.

Just like the shock, the fork has four possible adjustments, but you can only see two of them.

- Make a note of your setting in your race log notebook. Don't have one (tsk, tsk)? Then use a Sharpie to write it on the frame where it won't get rubbed off by your boots or legs.

3. Low-speed Compression

Low-speed compression has nothing to do with bike speed, but how fast or slow the shock shaft is moving. Most of your shock compression adjustments are done with the low-speed compression adjuster rather than the high-speed.

- The low-speed compression adjuster is the one you adjust using a screwdriver—the screw inside the hex nut of the high-speed compression adjuster.
- Like the other settings, it's based on clicks in or out— in is stiffer, out is softer—measured from all the way in. When making an adjustment, first turn it all the way in and then count clicks as you turn it out.
- When you're in the small roller section or landing from jumps or drop-aways, pay attention to the response, as this is where the low-speed compression comes into play.
- Turning the screw IN will make the shock stiffer.
- Turning the screw OUT makes it softer.
- Test the action by going over some jumps and some rollers/whoops. If there's any bottoming, turn the low-speed compression clicker IN (stiffer) about two clicks and then retest.
- Repeat testing and resetting the low-speed compression clicker until the bottoming stops.
- Write down your settings in your logbook.

4. High-speed Compression

High-speed compression, again, has nothing to do with motorcycle speed. It's all about shock shaft speed.

- The high-speed compression adjuster is usually the large hex nut or dial.
- The high-speed adjuster has no detents so the setting is listed in full and partial turns of the adjuster.
- Turning the high-speed compression adjuster IN makes it stiff; turning it OUT softens the compression damping.
- The high-speed compression comes into play with square-edged bumps, the tops of whoops, and slap-down landings.
- Turning the high-speed adjuster IN increases the shock damping and makes the rear of the bike ride a bit higher.
- Turning the adjuster OUT softens the damping and lowers the ride height.
- Typically the actual range of adjustment on the high-speed compression adjuster is limited to about three turns.
- You shouldn't have to spend a lot of time adjusting the high-speed compression to get the rear end working properly.

FORK WIZARDRY

Like the shock, modern forks also have four built-in possible tuning adjustments. Learning how to use them—and when—can make the difference between a sweet handling bike and a barge. However, only two of the adjusters are easily and quickly accessible. The adjustments are:

1. Spring rate
2. Oil height
3. Rebound damping
4. Compression damping

1. Spring Rate

Fork spring rate is the least understood and most confusing aspect of fork tuning, although a good tuner can sort it out quickly. Cutting to the chase:

- In an effort to make everyone happy, the manufacturers typically set up the forks with too soft a spring and a too-high oil height. This is a compromise to accommodate a wide range of rider sizes, speeds, and abilities. Like all compromises, it's rarely the best choice.
- If you have to turn the compression adjuster all the way in to stop the fork from bottoming, you need stiffer fork springs.
- Only the very lightest riders will need softer fork springs.
- When you first send out the forks to be revalved, expect to hear ". . . you need new springs." The OEM springs aren't worn out; they're just the wrong ones for best performance.

2. Oil Height

Oil height refers to the liquid spring inside your forks. Fork oil is the lubricant that flows through the shims and valves of your forks. It is also a somewhat adjustable factor. By measuring and adjusting the height of the oil, you affect the air space above the oil. This air space functions as a spring.

- More oil = stiffer (less air spring effect)
- Less oil = softer (more air space, more air spring effect)
- You can add or siphon out small amounts of oil through the bleeder valve at the top of the forks. Motion Pro makes a tool that allows you to precisely measure fork oil added or removed.
- An easy way to make better use of the tuning capabilities of the "air spring" is via separate reservoirs that plug into the fork cap bleeder screws. By increasing the available air volume in the fork and adjusting the compressed air that's present, you can easily control how soft or stiff the forks feel over small and intermediate bumps. Front wheel tracking also is typically improved. Easy to install—30 minutes, tops—they cost about $250 to $300 and many pro riders use them. AirCells is one good brand.
- Your first fork oil change should be after about 10 hours for a new bike. This allows time for the suspension to break in. Stock fork oils typically are mediocre at best. Have them changed early in the game and then every 20 hours riding time thereafter.

3. Rebound Damping

As with shock rebound, this refers to how quickly the fork returns to fully extended after landing from a jump or hitting a bump.

- If rebound is too quick, the bike pogos up and down.
- If the rebound is too slow, the bike won't extend quickly enough to be ready for the next bump, and you hit the next obstacle with the available suspension travel already used up—this is referred to as "packing."
- The rebound adjuster is located at either the top of the forks or at the bottom, depending on the manufacturer. Adjust with a flat-blade screwdriver.
- Turning the rebound screw IN slows the rebound.
- Turning the rebound screw OUT speeds up the rebound.
- As with other suspension settings, write down your settings in your logbook. You *are* keeping a logbook, right?

The easy way to measure and adjust fork oil levels is with a syringe unit such as this version from Motion Pro. You need something that will fit the bleed valve on top of the forks.

EVERY SUSPENSION IS DIFFERENT

Magazines and manufacturers publish their guidelines on what the correct settings should be for your weight, speed, and other factors. But these guidelines are only a starting point. There is enough manufacturing tolerance between two otherwise identical shocks where settings that work on one won't work on the other.

Sometimes it's pretty easy to tell that your suspension needs attention.

4. Compression Damping

The compression adjuster slows or speeds how quickly the forks compress (obviously).

- The adjuster will be either on the top or the bottom of the fork, depending on the brand. If on top, don't confuse it with the air pressure release screw. As always, refer to your manual.
- The compression adjuster affects the forks from mid-stroke to fully compressed; not the early portion of fork travel.
- Turn the adjuster IN (clockwise) with a flat-blade screwdriver to make the forks stiffer; OUT to make them softer.
- If the compression adjuster is at the top of the forks, instead of using a screwdriver, you can install aftermarket pieces that let you adjust compression by hand—a nice convenience when you're trying to dial in the forks for the day.
- If the forks aren't getting full travel, turn the compression adjuster OUT.
- You can easily measure fork travel by putting a zip-tie on the tube and going for a ride. The zip-tie will show the full stroke and is a quick visual tuning aid. You want the zip-tie to end up within the last 2 to 4cm of the fork.

HOW TO SHIP YOUR SUSPENSION

Shipping off your suspension sounds simple enough, but there are some gotchas. Do it this way:

- Take this seriously. Your suspension components are worth a couple thousand dollars.
- Get the right box. It's not always easy to find one that's both long enough and sturdy enough. The bigger suspension shops will usually offer a special box they'll send to you.
- Buy some bubble wrap and package tape. Wrap each fork leg individually. Don't use paper and don't wrap the fork legs together; they'll get banged up in shipping.
- Ditto on the shock; lots of bubble wrap. Put the shock in with the fork legs and fill the box with packing paper or foam peanuts.
- Include an envelope with your name and contact information, plus details on your weight, riding ability, skill level, and any related information. Don't fudge on either your weight (dressed to ride) or your ability. You'll probably need to include your credit card information as well.
- Ship via UPS or FedEx so there is tracking information.
- Insure your box for $2,000 (really).
- When your renewed suspension pieces come back, save the box for shipping them back when the fluids need freshening.
- Local suspension tuning shops vary quite a bit in quality; some are excellent, most are good, and a few are not worth the bother. Advantages of local shops is that going back for service or fine-tuning is more convenient; they know (or should know) the local tracks and local conditions, and they're often at the same races you're at and can help get things dialed in. Ask around among your racing friends about local shops and see what their experiences have been like.

The rebound adjuster is usually buried at the bottom of one fork leg and is easy to forget about. Don't.

The compression adjuster can be easy to confuse with the air pressure release screw. There are aftermarket adjusters that make it easier to adjust compression with no tools necessary.

The good suspension shops will put a sticker on the pieces identifying things like spring weight, oil level, and other tuning details to make trackside adjustments easier.

Trackside Suspension Cheat Sheet

Hard Pack/Blue Groove	Adjust compression as soft as possible to handle square-edged bumps.
Loamy Terrain	Adjust a little stiffer for the soft sections and jumps. Think "intermediate" for your settings.
Soft/Sandy/Muddy	Stiffen fork compression and shock rebound so the bike rides on top of the terrain and can deal with the added weight of mud.
Rocky/Rooty	Go very soft on the compression to absorb the sharp hits. Soften rebound so the bike is responsive.

If you don't have a logbook to record your settings, start one. In the meantime, write the setting with a Sharpie on a part of the frame or the shock itself.

WHAT THE SUSPENSION IS TELLING YOU

One of the reasons so few riders have their suspension properly dialed-in is that they simply don't understand the messages being sent their way, so they don't know where or what to adjust. Some things you need to know:

- Only change one thing at a time; otherwise you have no idea what fixed or made the problem worse.
- Learn how to test your suspension. See the next section.
- Write down what you've done in your logbook immediately or else you'll be more confused and further away from the fix.
- Sometimes the fork's problems are coming from the shock and vice-versa.
- You're attempting to attain a level and balanced suspension platform. If one end is considerably out of whack, the other end will be affected as well.
- Any time you reach the outer boundaries of adjusting, suspect that you may be dealing with the valving or with spring rate problems.
- No amount of clicker twisting or other fiddling will fix components that are worn out, leaking, damaged, or fighting against rusted linkage and swingarm bearings.
- Refer to your manual so you know you're tweaking the adjusters in the correct direction.

HOW TO TEST YOUR SUSPENSION

Part of the problem in deciphering your suspension's messages is that the rider often has a hard time feeling exactly what is going on. Here are the rules of testing in order to sort out your suspension and get it zeroed in:

- Know how things work. What you've read so far is a good starting point.
- I repeat: Never change more than one factor at a time. Otherwise you won't know what is affecting what.
- Write everything down. Keep a logbook in your toolbox and use it. Or at least use those blank pages in the back of

your owner's manual to record your numbers.
- Bring a friend—preferably another rider—to watch. The watcher can often see things that the rider cannot sense. Buy a small handheld video cam and have your friend record the test sessions for review.
- When in doubt, return to your stock or personal baseline settings and start over. It is one more reason to keep a log book.
- Test in the parts of the track where you're having problems—you don't have to ride the whole track if the problem you're chasing is only happening at one jump or roller section.
- Run the same lines every time at near-race speed.
- Suspension testing takes time and discipline, so don't attempt it during a race. Race days are just for minor fine tuning.

MAKING YOUR SUSPENSION BETTER

You can only go as fast as the suspension will allow, so money spent here is well worth it. Beyond simply finding a pro suspension shop you trust, some of your options include:

- **AirCells** are separate subtanks (reservoirs) mounted to the forks with lines running to the fork caps. The increased air volume of the subtanks allows the

WATCH THE SHOCK BUMPER

When working on your rear shock, be careful not to tear the rubber shock bumper. It functions as an extra spring when the shock is at full travel, and if it gets torn (were you prying around with a screwdriver, maybe?) the shock will bottom out. A torn shock bumper has to be replaced; it can't be repaired.

SUSPENSION CHEAT SHEETZ®

FORKS	CHECK FOR/DO THIS:
Feel too harsh	Correct spring rate? Turn the compression OUT two clicks. Too high oil height Worn out fork internals
Fork bottoms out	Increase compression (IN) two clicks, retest. If you run out of adjustments, the spring is too soft. Correct spring rate? Too low oil height. Add 5cc (no more than that)
Head shake at speed	If it's bottoming, increase compression as above Slide the forks down in the clamps Go a click or two OUT (softer) on rebound Check steering head bearings for grease and a slight amount of preload Fork springs are too stiff
Forks are harsh	Too much compression damping; Go OUT a click, retest Too much rebound damping, causing "packing" holding the forks down in a stiffer area of travel. Soften (go OUT) a click or two. Fork binding. Center the fork.
Front end knifes in	If the fork is bottoming, do as directed above Go IN (stiffen) a click or two on the shock's (not the fork's) rebound Go OUT (soften) a click on the shock's preload May need stiffer fork spring
Bike won't turn	Go IN a click or two on the shock's (not the fork's) preload to stiffen Slide forks UP in the triple clamps Increase fork's rebound (go IN) a click or two and retest Decrease (go OUT) on the fork's compression Reduce (go OUT) a click on fork rebound Increase (go IN) one click on the shock's low-speed compression

REAR SHOCK	CHECK FOR/DO THIS:
Rear end kicks up	Too much rebound; go OUT (soften) two clicks Check static sag; too little causes this; adjust and retest Forks are too soft (dives too much on braking); go IN on fork compression
Hates the whoops	Go IN on high-speed compression damping one click, retest Increase (go IN) rebound damping a click or two, retest
Rear end not hooking up	Check race and static sag; not enough preload can cause this; adjust Reduce rebound (OUT on the clickers) to get the wheel back on the ground faster Check rear axle position—it may be too far back; shorten chain If this occurs in rocks/roots, go OUT on the high-speed compression Shock may be worn out or need revalving and fresh fluid
Rear end bottoms out	Lack of compression. Increase (IN on clickers) low-speed compression Increase (ditto) high-speed compression Increase spring preload (less rider sag) by no more than 5mm Decrease (OUT on clickers) rebound damping Too soft of spring If the components have a lot of time on them, they need a rebuild/service
Kicks side to side	Too much compression damping. Go OUT a click on low-speed compression Too much rebound damping. Go OUT a click

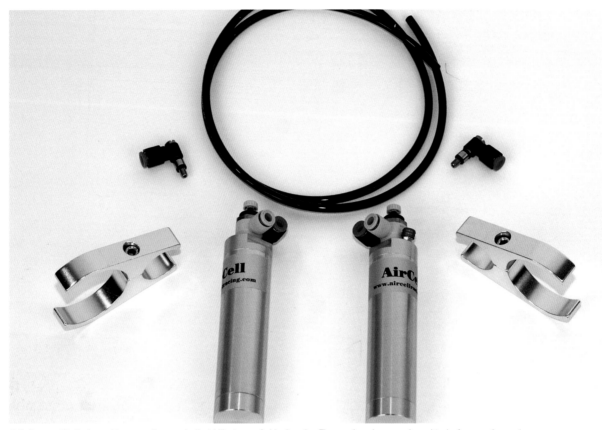

AirCells are subtanks to provide more volume and adjustability to your fork's air spring. The pros have been running subtanks for years for good reason.

suspension to be plusher over the little stuff, while at high speeds the system makes the forks stiffer. Subtanks add more tuning options while reducing harshness and improving front wheel tracking and cornering. Installation is simple and costs about $250 to $300 at www.AirCellracing.com. The pros have been running subtanks for years because they improve even heavily modified factory forks. A variation on this concept is the TGT suspension handlebar which uses the hollow cross-section of the handlebar as the subtank. Cost is $240 at www.tgtracing.com.

- **Adjust the wheelbase.** Lengthening or shortening the wheelbase affects both handling and suspension action. Shortening the chain and moving the axle forward makes the bike turn quicker and makes the rear suspension stiffer. A longer wheelbase turns slower and tracks smoother over rough terrain.

- **Steering damper** is the speed secret you may never have considered. Factory racers use them, even if you can't readily see them. A steering damper can help cure a bike that oversteers or suffers from head shake. A steering damper reduces arm pump and lets you go faster because you're not constantly fighting the handlebars. A steering stabilizer reduces front wheel deflection—what happens when the wheel hits an obstacle that tries to

throw it off the line—and is the secret weapon for speed in sandy, rocky, rooty conditions. Heck, it's a secret weapon in any racing situation and it's definitely not just for the off-road guys. Get one! One nice thing about buying a steering stabilizer is that it's an investment that pays off for many years because you can move it from bike to bike as you change scoots. The only thing that has to be changed is the mounting hardware—the stabilizer stays the same. The brand name most associated with these is Scotts and one will set you back about $400, but again, you'll be able to transfer it to every new bike you get and the units are completely rebuildable so it's a one-time purchase.

- **Triple clamps.** Aftermarket triple clamps offer a more rigid mounting point for your front suspension and you can also change the offset to change the steering responses. If you race primarily on tight tracks, you may want less offset in order to make the bike turn quicker. Race the desert? Then the opposite may be true. While you can buy just the top or bottom clamps, to change the offset you need both. It's also generally easier to purchase both clamps with the steering stem already installed, which saves you the hassle of needing a hydraulic press to remove and then refit the stem in the new clamps.

GREASE YOUR BALLS (BEARINGS)

Neglecting the bearings that the suspension components rely on should be a criminal offense. It's really just basic maintenance and, as detailed in Chapter 2, it's one of the first things you do with any bike, new or used.

All it takes is some time, a tub of waterproof grease, and the owner's manual. No super-specialized tools or mechanical ability are required. Neglecting these components can lead to seized swingarm pivots (a nasty problem to try to fix), poor suspension action, bad handling, and expensive repairs. Here's what you need to know:

- The more often you use a pressure washer, the more often you need to check and regrease suspension bearings. The high-pressure water stream blows seals open, drives out grease, drives dirt in deeper, and leaves water behind to corrode parts.
- The aftermarket makes it easy to maintain and replace your suspension bearings by offering complete kits with good instructions. PivotWorks and All Balls are the names to look for. You'll have everything you need—seals, bearings, and instructions.
- Keep your hands clean when greasing things up. Huh? What I mean is don't mix a load of dirt from your hands in with the grease you're applying. Wear nitrile gloves and wipe them clean with paper towels.

A steering damper/stabilizer gives the forks better manners and ends the wrestling match you're having with the handlebars. Not cheap, but you can transfer them to each new bike you buy—and you will want to.

Aftermarket triple clamps are more rigid and reduce fork flex. You can also use them to change fork offset to make the bike turn faster or slower.

LEAKING FORK SEALS

It's a common bit of advice in magazines and online to use a feeler gauge or business card to clear out debris from under the fork seals. However, this is only a temporary fix when you find yourself with a leaking fork seal. Dislodging the debris may stop or slow the leak, but you haven't actually fixed the problem, and in the process you have probably pushed dirt up into the fork where it can do some real damage. Fork seals wear out, so either learn how to replace them yourself or periodically have them replaced when you have the fork serviced. Replace seals and wipers as a set. Dirt defense is the wiper's job; the seal's is to keep oil in, not keep dirt out.

Sliding a feeler gauge or bit of stiff plastic under the fork seal to clear out dirt may temporarily stop a leak, but it's not a fix. Plan on replacing seals and wipers regularly.

Spend some quality time cleaning, inspecting, and regreasing your suspension. It's time well spent.

Use high quality waterproof grease and work it into the bearings. Make sure the parts are clean before you start greasing them up. If you want your hands to stay clean, put on a pair of nitrile gloves.

- Use the right stuff. Your manual will have specifics, but a good motorcycle waterproof grease generally meets the bill. A lithium-based grease is also good.
- Do it all: linkage, swingarm, and steering head. It's easy to do one or another and then put the rest off. It's better to check and do them all at the same time so you know they've been done.
- LOOK at the bearings when you take them out. Look for flat spots, corrosion, and galling; replace if you find any of these conditions.
- Clean out any dirt before applying grease. Dumping grease on top of dirt just traps it inside. You want clean parts before you start greasing them up.
- When installing the rear shock, lift the rear wheel up when tightening the shock bolt. If you don't do it this way, it can throw off your sag measurements.
- Wheel bearings are typically sealed and don't require grease.

WHY YOU NEED A HOLESHOT DEVICE

While a holeshot device doesn't come with a guarantee that it'll catapult you to the front of the pack, if you race moto, you need one. Think of it as a cheap suspension modification, although a very narrowly focused one.

A holeshot device pulls the front forks down, shifting the weight bias forward, making the bike less likely to wheelie off the line. This makes it easier for the rider to dial in maximum forward thrust without worrying about his front fender kissing the sky. They release as soon as the fork compresses—when you get on the brakes, for example. Some tips:

- Unless you have the two-pin variety, holeshot devices only work on dirt start lines, not concrete. The two-pin style doesn't pull the forks down as far, so they may help on concrete starts.
- Are you short? A holeshot device makes it easier for short guys to get their feet down at the start.
- Most brands come with templates to help position the device correctly on the fork guard during installation, but if you can't find it, the working number is 3 to 4 inches down from the bottom of the fork tube.
- Some brands (Dirt Freak and UFO) save you the hassle of measuring, drilling, and pulling off the fork leg by offering holeshot devices built into new fork guards and a hinged fork mount.

CENTERING THE FRONT WHEEL

It sounds simple and boring, but centering the front wheel is how you make sure you're getting proper, bind-free fork action. A lot of riders do it all wrong. Here's how to do it correctly:

- Put the front wheel back in place and slide the axle into place, tightening the left side axle drop out bolts (the left side bolts as you face the front of the bike).

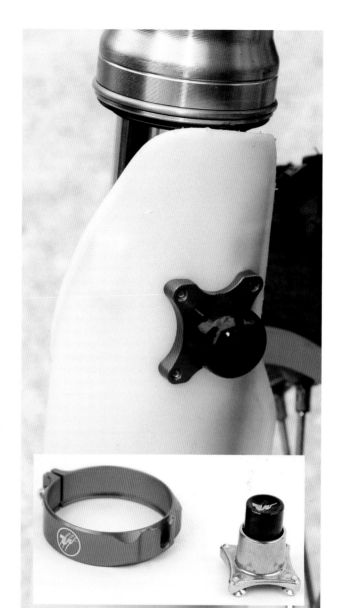

Think of a holeshot device as a part of the suspension package—because it is. It keeps the forks under compression, so you're less likely to wheelie coming out of the gate. If you race motocross, you need one.

- Now tighten the axle nut, leaving the right side drop out bolts loose.
- Now go back to the left side (again, facing the front of the bike) and loosen the drop out bolts again.
- Back to the right side drop outs and tighten those two bolts.
- Now comes the "centering" part of all this. Either spin the front wheel several times and grab the front brake until the axle finds center on the axle or push the foot of the fork in and out until it's centered.
- Now tighten up the left side drop out bolts and you're done.

Chapter 5
Ergos: Making It Fit

WHEN IT FITS, YOU'RE FASTER AND MORE CONFIDENT

When your shoes are the wrong size, your feet hurt, you get blisters, and you can't run or walk as fast as usual. You're distracted, in a bad mood, and focused on your discomfort rather than on what you're doing.

The same bad things happen when your bike doesn't fit properly. When you're trying to keep a 50-horsepower moto-missile pointed in the right direction, discomfort is not a good thing. Cue the music for a dramatic crash and burn video. This is why it's hard to get on a buddy's bike and ride it as fast as you know you can—it's set up for him, not you.

Motorcycles are a design compromise, built to fit a mythical "average rider." Chances are very good that this guy isn't anything like you. Getting your bike to fit properly should be a priority.

WHAT IS PROPER FIT AND FEEL?

There's no simple answer to the fit and feel question. Everyone is built differently, and what works for Ricky Carmichael or James Stewart or your best friend probably isn't going to work for you.

Proper bike setup means tailoring your machine to match you and nobody else. Don't let your buddies tell you what is and isn't right. Your bike only has to fit one person: you.

Your goal is to adjust the bike so everything falls naturally to hand, your movements are smooth, your boot always catches the shift lever, and you can feather the rear brake pedal perfectly and never stall out. When you've tailored the bike, you move fluidly between sitting, standing, or attack position, expending minimal energy and always feeling in control. It's the difference between buying clothes off the rack and wearing something professionally tailored.

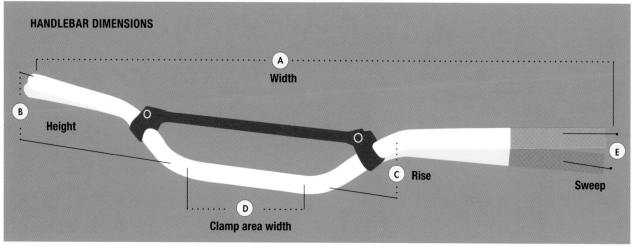

HANDLEBAR DIMENSIONS

A — Width
B — Height
C — Rise
D — Clamp area width
E — Sweep

There are only about a half-dozen distinctly different handlebar bends. What you're most concerned about is height, width, and sweep. What works best? Experiment to find out.

Achieving this ergonomic perfection means experimenting, replacing, or adjusting all the points of contact with the bike: handlebars, seat, pegs, and controls. Let's start at the top.

BAR BASICS

There's a lot of engineering hidden inside that supposedly simple metal tubing; it's how you stay in control, so treat it with respect. What you need to know:

- Steel bars have one redeeming quality: low cost. For the bucks-down play rider, they're a reasonable choice if only because they're cheap. If you race, you need aluminum for the added strength.
- Oversize bars are much harder to bend and suck up more shocks and vibes than standard $7/8$-inch (22mm) bars. If you're running standard size bars and your hands are tingling after a ride, switching to oversize 1-$1/8$ inch (30mm ProTaper–style) bars will probably help. Oversize bars require either a universal adapter (about $50) that bolts onto your existing clamps, a set of bar mounts for oversize bars (about $75), or a new top triple clamp with oversize mounts ($200-plus).
- Never try to save a few bucks by attempting to straighten a bent bar. Handlebars are consumables like tires, so replace it whenever it gets bent or has any type of deep cut, crack, or visible surface stress.
- There are really only about a half-dozen different motocross handlebar bends and about three of them are the main sellers. Most of the bends, especially the rider-signature models, vary only a couple millimeters in dimensions and few riders can detect a difference from one bend to another. Signature model bars won't make you any faster.
- Want a bar bend that's all-around good? Go with any version of a high-CR if you're tall. Short? Choose the low-CR version.

- The wrong handlebar can make you a lousy racer. If it's too low, too wide, too tall, has too much sweep or not enough, you'll feel it in your wrists and shoulders, have a hard time making the sitting-to-standing transition, and never really feel in control. Experiment with different bar bends (try your buddies' bikes) and bar positions. Too many riders treat the stock handlebar as something they just have to get used to. That's dead wrong. The handlebar is where you start when fitting the bike to your personal dimensions.
- If the bars don't come with position reference marks engraved, use a permanent marker to add some.
- While you're experimenting with bars, try out different bar positions in the clamps by rotating it forward or back. Since modern race bikes are ridden body-forward in the attack position, the best bar position may be quite a bit forward.
- Never adjust bar position while seated, unless you never intend to stand up.
- Aftermarket top triple clamps with multiple bar positions and bar mounts that are taller and shorter than stock are widely available, so there's no excuse for not getting something as critical as bar position nailed down. Yes, you'll have to invest some money; yes, it will be worth it.
- The unique FasstFlexx handlebars combine adjustable and replaceable sections with a vibration and shock-absorbing dampening system. If you have a hard time finding standard bars that fit or have wrist problems such as carpel tunnel syndrome, the FasstFlexx bars are what you need. They are expensive (over $200) but well worth it.
- A new bike may require a different bar bend than what you've been using, so just because your favorite bars worked great on your last bike doesn't mean the same bar is the right one for the new bike.

Some bar mounts have an arrow or other mark indicating the front of the mount; look for it. When tightening the bar mounts, tighten the front bolts first and the rear bolts last. This stretches the clamp over the handlebars so the bar won't rotate even with a hard landing.

ASV levers are spring-loaded so they're they'll flip back if bent. Pricey but they can save your riding day.

NOTCHED LEVERS

KTM and some aftermarket levers come with a notch about a third of a way from the end. The notch allows the lever to break at the notch in the event of a crash, rather than destroying the whole lever. If you're far from the truck, one of these notched levers can be a day-saver. You can make your own notches by drilling a small hole through your lever a couple of inches up from the end.

Installing New Handlebars

Like most things in life, there's a right way and wrong way to do this.

- Check the bar clamps for sharp metal burrs. Chamfer the clamps with a round file to remove sharp edges so they don't cut into the bar in a bad crash.
- Clamps often have a "front" position, usually marked with an arrow or dot. Be sure it's facing the right way.
- Tighten the front clamp bolts first and then the rear clamp bolts.
- The reason you install the front bolts first is to pinch the bars in the clamps so they won't rotate even on a hard landing. The clamp is stretched tight over the bar.

CONTROLS WHERE YOU NEED THEM

Do you have big paws or small ones? Long fingers or stubs? Get control levers that match what Mother Nature gave you. To use myself as an example, while I'm tall with gangly arms and legs, my fingers are short, making it difficult to comfortably have two fingers on some lever designs.

There are a lot of aftermarket lever assemblies available with a wide range of features, lever shapes, and lengths, so experiment to find what matches up best with your hands. Most good lever assemblies include adjustment screws to move the lever closer or further away—if yours don't, get new ones. If you have long fingers, you can probably use any lever from anybody, but if you find yourself straining to stab the levers while riding, try other brands and designs.

Shopping for levers isn't just about size and shape. You also get to choose between regular levers or pivoting (folding) designs that are spring-loaded and fold under impact. Pivoting levers will survive most crashes, are available for both sides of the bars, and while initially more expensive, they quickly pay for themselves. ASV is the original creator of hinged levers and its levers are still the best.

Always opt for premium versions of lever assemblies as pioneered by Works Connection with bearings in the lever pivot and a Teflon sleeve that allows the assembly to move on impact. A lever with a bearing is noticeably smoother and can make the difference between feeding in just enough clutch for a holeshot or finding yourself buried mid-pack.

Levers require maintenance. They wear out and get sloppy, especially the clutch. Lubricate the lever pivots, adjust the play, and if the lever has become worn, floppy, or bent, replace it. Adjust lever play per the manual. Too much play will cause the clutch to slip.

Mount levers so the ball end doesn't stick out past the end of the handlebar or the first crash will snap off the lever.

If you ride enduros or trail ride through the trees, install aluminum handguards (a.k.a. Bark Busters) or at the minimum, plastic guards.

On the Gas

Your most intimate and important connection with your bike is through your right wrist. It's where the good times begin.

The one big flaw of most stock throttles is that the inner throttle tube is plastic and breaks easily in even a minor crash. That will put a quick end to your riding. Some solutions:

- Billet aluminum throttle tubes can take a licking and . . . well, you know the rest. These machined aluminum tubes won't break in any crash you're likely to walk away from. Make it one of the first things on your shopping list.
- There are some gotchas to billet throttle tubes, though. Buy a good one, a brand name you recognize, and check for fit. If you feel any binding or burrs, take it back for a refund. The hard anodizing color on the billet tubes isn't for looks—it's lubrication to keep aluminum from rubbing directly on aluminum. Some versions come with Teflon strips to further lubricate and make the movement easy.
- Install the tube with some dry graphite so it spins freely.
- If you run Bark Buster–style handguards, be sure to get a throttle tube that has a removable end cap, as not all do.
- When installing any throttle, don't butt it up completely against the end of the handlebar. Slide it on so it's up against the handlebar end, then back it out about 1/8-inch so it turns without binding or scraping.
- Throttle tube assemblies work best when clean and dry. On a regular basis, disassemble the throttle and clean it and the handlebar area thoroughly with contact cleaner. Check for any burrs in the metal and file them off.
- Most types of lubricant gum things up but one acceptable lubricant is dry graphite powder. Apply it lightly and be sure you don't have any of the graphite underneath the clamping area.
- Four-stroke bikes have dual cables and a heftier throttle action that can be tiring. One solution is a metal throttle tube with an inner bearing that makes the throttle action smoother. WPS and Sunline are some sources for these throttles. A little more expensive (typically around $75) than plain billet throttles, their smooth action makes them worth it.

Get a Grip!

Grips are a personal thing and a fashion statement. There are dozens of colors, sizes, designs, and styles, so indulge yourself and try some variations until you find a favorite.

- Match grips to your hand size. Thick grips for big hands, thinner ones for small mitts.
- Grips wear out from the friction between your gloves and the grip, plus the crash damage any dirt bike suffers. Grips are cheap so freshen up the bike with new ones at regular intervals.
- Dual-compound grips have a softer section to absorb

Good levers make a difference, especially on the starts where smooth action translates into a smooth launch. The Works Connection Elite Pro Perch is the premier clutch lever assembly.

Install the levers so they don't extend past the end of the handlebar. If they stick out too far, they're the first thing to hit the ground.

A billet throttle tube can save your riding day. It is $60 worth of cheap insurance. Unlike the stock throttle tubes, a billet tube won't crack in a crash.

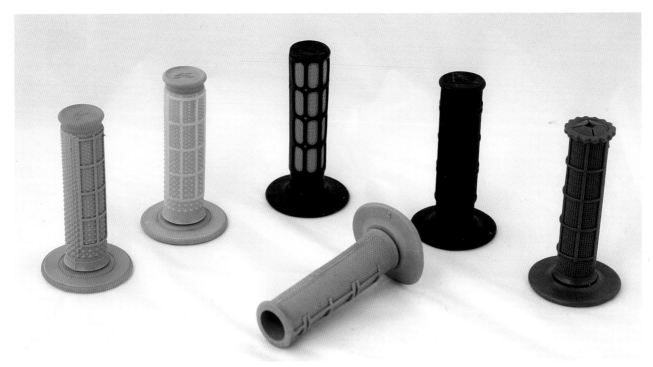

There are grips to fit every size and shape of paw. Experiment until you find what works.

A grip donut keeps your thumb from being turned into hamburger.

CABLE ROUTING

When swapping handlebars around it's easy to misroute the cables. That's why you need to refer to your owner's manual to be sure you have things in the right place, especially in relation to the front number plate. Failing to check this can lead to clutch and throttle problems and a crash.

vibes and shocks matched up with a tougher outer section for a longer life. Dual-compound grips work, but not every rider likes the feel. Again, you need to try a few different brands before you make up your mind.

- Kevlar-reinforced grips with a dual compound are the latest refinement, producing a grip that lasts longer. Renthal makes these and yes, they cost a bit more. Personal experience with them is that yes, they do last a lot longer.

- If you frequently get arm-pump, experiment with different shapes of grips and bar bends. Look for tapered grips which are thinner at one end. It may be all you need to fix the problem.

Installing Grips

There are plenty of ways to install grips and many people claim their special method is best. Personally, I've never had the guts to see if some of these tricks (hair spray?) really will hold the grips in place or whether they'll come off in mid-air. Why risk it? Here are five methods that DO work:

- Grip Glue: When you buy grips, buy grip glue. Have some extra on hand as you'll use it. Grip glue is simple, quick, and—most importantly—it works. Spread three thick beads on the bar and a circle inside the grip. Slide the grip on quickly and rotate into position. The grip glue acts as a lubricant to help get the grip onto the bar. Grip glue needs to dry overnight and some grips, especially Renthals, are picky about the brand of grip glue and will tear if the wrong product is used. Annoying but true.

- Super Glue: This does what super glues (cyanoacrylate) do: It dries super fast. ProTaper offers one brand, but it's basically just gel-type super glue. Keep some in your toolbox along with a spare set of grips. Super glue sets up in minutes, meaning you can replace grips and get back on the track that same day.
- Cloth Electrical Tape: This is an old school method that's cheap and effective. Use the kind of tape that's sticky black cloth (not vinyl) and wrap a layer around the bar end. Give it a spray of contact cleaner and slide the grip on. As soon as the contact cleaner evaporates, the grip is locked in place. Do not use gasoline to wet the tape.
- Gorilla Snot: Otherwise known as automotive weather strip cement. You can get it from an auto parts store. Designed to hold automotive rubber weather stripping in place, it works fine in this simpler role. Spread some on as described previously for grip glue.
- Spray Paint: Use clear spray enamel and apply to the bar and slide the grip on. Krylon is the preferred brand. Use enamel only.
- Before applying any glue, cover the hole in the throttle tube with a piece of duct tape so glue doesn't get inside the throttle.
- Prick the end of the grip with a razor knife if the seal is too tight and you can't get the grip to slide on completely.
- Unless you're using super glue, install new grips at least the day before you ride because the glue needs time to dry. Don't replace grips on race day unless it's an emergency.
- Use two pieces of safety wire in the grooves on the grip. Install the safety wire immediately after installing the grip while the adhesive is still setting up. Cut off the wire ends and bend them into the grip with a screwdriver tip so they won't snag your hand.
- Before installing the grip, put a piece of rag or foam rubber inside the open end of the handlebar on the clutch side. This keeps any dirt that might get inside from a torn grip from migrating to the throttle and jamming things up.
- When you know you're going to be riding in wet conditions, apply more glue than normal so that some oozes out where the grip meets the handlebar. When cleaning up the overflow, leave a bead at the grip/bar junction to seal it so water can't get in. Or apply silicone seal to seal this spot and keep water out.
- As necessary, tailor your grips to conform to your hand. A razor blade can trim ridges on the grip to better match your mitts.

CUTTING TO THE CHASE

Need to cut a handlebar down to size because it's too wide? Instead of using a hacksaw which leaves a ragged, angled cut, use a plumbing tubing cutter. Any hardware store has these tools for a few dollars and it'll cut through a handlebar leaving a clean, smooth and, most importantly, straight cut.

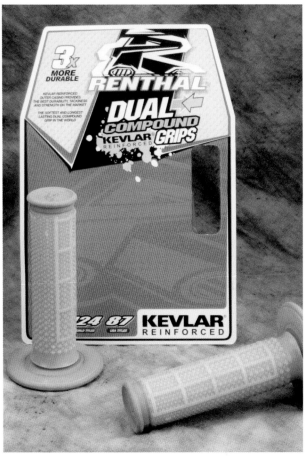

Grips wear out, some of them quite quickly. The Renthal Kevlar grips use a Kevlar compound to lengthen their life—and it seems to work. I've put a full season on one pair that shows little wear, yet they're still providing good grip and cushioning.

Five products to use when installing grips: (1) grip glue (2) friction tape and contact cleaner (3) gel-type super glue (4) automotive weather strip adhesive and (5) clear spray enamel paint, preferably Krylon. Forget about anything else; these are what work.

Start with clean handlebars. Scrape off or use mineral spirits to remove old adhesive—use acetone if removing old super glue. Plug the clutch end of the handlebar with a piece of coarse foam to keep dirt from getting in. Put a piece of tape over the open end of a throttle to keep glue from getting inside.

Spread three thick beads of grip glue on the bar and another bead inside the grip. Slide the grips on and quickly twist into the desired position. If you're using super glue adhesive, you will have only seconds to do this.

Wrap some safety wire around the grooves on the grip and tighten. Safety wire pliers are nice for this, but regular pliers work fine. Wipe up any oozing glue and let the adhesive set up overnight before riding unless you used super glue.

When it comes to footpegs, BIG is better. Here's stock alongside aftermarket.

Grip Removal

- If you're not going to reuse the grips, cut them off with a razor knife—it's the quick and easy way.
- No knife? Pry a corner up with a screwdriver and squirt brake cleaner under the grip to melt the adhesive so you can tug it off.
- If you want to reuse it, crank up your air compressor with a nozzle attachment and blow the grip off. Insert a screwdriver where the grip meets the bar so you can get the air nozzle in.
- Whenever you remove grips, use some mineral spirits or brake cleaner to remove the old glue left behind. If you used super glue, then you'll need acetone to remove the old glue. Some nail polish removers have this in them, some don't.

ON YOUR FEET!

Be fussy when it comes to footpegs. Make sure they're big, wide, and bristling with plenty of sharp teeth. Hardly any stock peg meets those specs. Good aftermarket choices are:

- Pivoting Pegs: Having a hard time getting your toe under the shifter, no matter how much you play around with its position? The solution is a set of pivoting pegs that rock back and forth in response to your body weight. You never notice the pegs' small movements, but you will definitely notice that you're no longer missing shifts and

that the brake pedal is always exactly where it should be. Because the pegs move in response to your body position, your feet stay planted and the teeth on the pegs don't need to be so aggressive and tear up your boot soles. Pivoting footpegs can be hard to find, so you may have to special order, but they're well worth it. Prices average around $125. They are made for specific models of bikes so you can find your brand by surfing to www.pivotpegz.com.

Pivoting pegs rotate a few degrees back and forth to match your body position as you move on the balls of your feet. This slight pivoting action puts your boots in the proper position to catch the shifter and brake pedal perfectly. Our experience is that they also reduce boot wear and help keep your feet planted better than conventional pegs.

67

SHARPENING FOOTPEGS

Sharp footpegs are essential. You want them aggressive so they bite into your boot sole and grip your feet under even the wost conditions. Tools to sharpen them are a flat file (slow but cheap), or a high-speed grinder (pricey but very fast). Sharpening the pegs should be part of your pre-race prep.

- Big Pegs: Most bikes come with petite pegs. Go big! Your boots need a wide, comfortable perch with aggressive teeth that grip your soles and let mud ooze out. Big pegs are insurance against having a boot slip off when things get hot and heavy. Sunline, Pro Circuit, Lightspeed, Moose Racing, and others all make good wide pegs. You need them.
- Look for designs that are taller in the middle than on the sides. This slight arch allows your feet to rock forward and back on the pegs, matching your body movement.
- Titanium footpegs are very cool looking, very expensive, and provide zero real-world benefit.

SHIFTER BLUES

Stock shifters are fine if you have a body that's identical to whatever factory test rider was used as a baseline. Since races are won or lost based on hitting all your shifts cleanly (not to mention clearing the big jumps) if you're missing shifts, then you have a problem you need to fix. Assuming you have the clutch free-play properly adjusted and there's no mechanical problem, play with the shift lever. Experiment with repositioning the shifter on the shaft—that's why it has all those splines—or even bending the lever to match your boots. If that doesn't fix the problem, check out aftermarket products from Sunline, Pro Circuit, Wirtz, and Hammerhead that offer slightly different lengths, shifter tip size, and bends.

SIZE DOES MATTER

Are you too short for your bike? Short riders and tall bikes can be a bad mix, so do some custom tailoring. Here are your options.

Fixes for Short Riders

- If you're short, cut down the seat, or replace it with a smaller seat from a different model or from an aftermarket source. To cut down the seat, pull out the staples that hold the cover in place and carefully cut down the foam with an electric carving knife—what you use to carve the turkey on Thanksgiving. Smooth the cuts with sandpaper, file, or grater from the kitchen. Take your time and don't go nuts with the carving or you'll find yourself sitting on the frame rails with every bump on the track tattooing your behind. Removing even a small amount of seat foam can make a big difference.

Big feet require longer shifters with wider contact points. The Hammerhead shifters are one favored brand, because you can choose from a variety of shifter tips to match your foot size.

A taller seat can make a huge difference in your riding position and overall comfort. Compare this SDG seat that's 1½ inches taller with the stocker.

- Pro riders who are short get the benefit of frames cut and welded to fit and the pegs relocated, but these are options that usually aren't available to the rest of us. TruTech in Corona, California, offers this service; www.trumoto.com.

- A cheaper way to improve things for the vertically challenged is to run pegs that are taller than stock. This takes some comparison shopping with tape measure in hand to find who's got the best dimensions, but it's worth it because even a small difference can be felt when riding. A welder can also make a set of pegs taller and beefier.

- The Fastway Evolution pegs have adjustable "teeth" (they're really set screws) that allow you to set up the height of the pegs from standard to lowboy positions. They're also about the widest pegs available.

- Just because you're short, don't assume that means you run the lowest, shortest bars you can find. The length of your arms and torso make a difference. Ricky Carmichael is well under skyscraper dimensions but runs relatively tall bars. Experiment with different bars until you can be like Goldilocks and say, ". . . it's just right."

- You might want to cut the bar width down a notch for more leverage if you feel like you're imitating a glider.

- You should be able to find handlebar mounts that are lower than stock; if you do, they're worth the price.

- Switch brands. Different bikes have different cockpit dimensions, so forget about your brand loyalties and see what fits you best. If you're comfortable, you'll be faster.

- Shorten the suspension. Suspension shops such as Factory Connection can shorten the front/rear suspension units for a very reasonable fee. You'll lose some suspension travel but will finally be able to touch the ground without the tippy-toe balancing act.

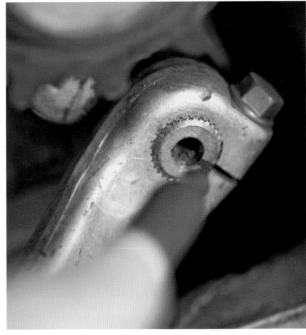

Before you move the shift lever to a new position on the shaft, use a Sharpie to make a reference mark so you can keep track of your changes.

THE NICKEL TRICK

When installing new grips, put a nickel in the left (clutch) side grip or glue it to the end of the handlebar before adding any grip glue. The coin will cover the end of the bar so that when (not if) you fall, the bar will push on the coin instead of the grip to keep it from ripping. That nickel can save you $15 for new grips. Only use this trick on the clutch side, not the throttle.

A step seat and a high-grip cover help keep you planted.

Fixes for Tall Riders

If you're a big galoot or the bike's cockpit is simply too cramped, do everything mentioned for the short riders except in reverse. That means a taller seat, tall bars (probably) in taller mounts, thinner pegs so your legs have some room, and probably a different shifter to accommodate your bigger boots.

OTHER TAILORING OPTIONS

- Add a step seat, especially if you're riding a 450cc bike. The step will help hold you in place under hard acceleration. You can make one yourself by adding a bump of foam glued to the seat about a foot from the back edge of the seat. Or you can purchase one ready-made from various sources.
- If the stock seat is too soft or too hard, experiment with seat foams. KTM is famous for having seats only slighter softer than granite, but a too-soft seat is also bad because you sink down into it.

- Gripper-style seat covers are now the rule, but some are better than others. Experiment to find out what works best for you.
- Small handguards keep rocky roost from smashing fingers, while warding off rain, mud, and cold. The downside is that in a crash, they can trap your fingers under the bar—I've got a kink in my pinky finger to prove it. The solution is either a handguard that has a soft rubber edge (Cyra makes one) or a version that rotates out of the way in a crash (Sunline for these).
- That bloody blister on your right thumb has a name: Yama-Thumb. The term was coined a couple decades ago courtesy of Yamaha's strange bar bend. The bar bend is the usual source of these blisters. Change the bars or install a set of grip donuts to provide some protective cushioning.
- If you find your boots or knee braces getting hung up on the bike's plastic, zip-tie the plastic down tighter, trim it with a razor knife, or use some duct tape to bridge any openings.

Chapter 6
Making It Look Good: Bodywork and Graphics

WE ALL LOVE EYE CANDY

One of the reasons we like riding dirt bikes is the chance to wear cool-looking gear and have trick-looking machines. We're gearheads and proud of it. A well-dressed bike may not be any faster, but it soothes our soul and ratchets up our self-confidence.

Since taste is something that we all have yet seldom can agree on, the only thing you really need to decide is what look matches your personality. The graphics companies offer a lot of options, from a factory race team-replica look to a totally custom approach using your own design.

Here's the scoop on making your bike look better, be more distinctive, and, on some levels, perform better in the bargain.

INSTALLING A NEW SEAT COVER

Seat covers get ripped, worn out, and faded with dirt burnished so deep into the vinyl it never looks clean. A new gripper seat cover adds color as well as the all-important "fanny traction," while also giving you an opportunity to make the seat taller or shorter. For about $40 to $60 it's a good place to start. Here's the step-by-step drill:

Looking good doesn't make you any faster. But it can't hurt. *Kawasaki Motors USA*

MAKE COLORED WHEELS LOOK LIKE NEW

Black wheels are the current fashion. They look cool when new, but a few rides in rocky terrain or a tire change and the black shows scars. You can fix it—if looks are that important to you—by using a permanent marker to cover up the scratches and scrapes. There are even some riders who have gotten tired of the regular silver rims and have used permanent markers to redo their wheels in another color; it works better than you might think.

Hide scratches and scars on colored wheels with a marker. It's not permanent, but it makes a great quickie fix.

- Take it out of the package, unfold it, and let it warm up in the sun or throw it in the clothes dryer for a few minutes. Warm vinyl stretches easier and makes the creases go away.
- Tools you'll need are an electric staple gun with short (1/4-inch or so) staples, a razor knife, scissors, a small flat-blade screwdriver, a needle-nose pliers (to remove old staples and misplaced new staples), and most important, a helper. You can install a seat cover flying solo, but a second person makes it quicker and simpler.
- Remove the old cover by prying out the staples with a needle-nose pliers and small screwdriver. You may also need to remove the seat mounts on some bikes if they bolt on.
- Position the cover on the seat with the seams lined up properly; staple the cover once or twice at the front.
- Switch ends, stretch the cover slightly, and staple twice at the back.

BLACK MARK REMOVAL

Your boots scuff things up, leaving black marks behind. Use mineral spirits to remove them. WD-40 may also work.

- Now work the sides, starting in front. Staple one side, then stretch the cover and staple the other side (this is where having a helper is important since you need three hands). Work side to side, headed toward the back, stretching the cover into place, and removing wrinkles.
- When you get near the seat mounts, use the razor knife and scissors to notch the cover so it fits around the mounts.
- When you arrive at the back of the seat, you may have to remove the staples you put there at the beginning in order to eliminate wrinkles and re-stretch the cover.
- With luck you have the seams in the right spot and there are no lumps or ridges. If so, do a final stapling run. If some adjustments are necessary, remove some staples, re-stretch, and staple again. Take your time and get it right.
- No matter how careful you are, you may still end up with a small wrinkle or two. Don't worry about it. They tend to work themselves out over time and it's hard to duplicate the flawless factory-applied seat covers, which are installed using a vacuum device that molds the seat cover in place.
- If there's a lot of excess material under the seat when you're done, use scissors or a razor knife to trim it away.
- You can always go back and re-stretch and reattach the seat cover if you're not satisfied with your first attempt.

Whatever look you want, one of the graphic companies can supply it. This is the Throttle Jockey Elsinore kit.

SHINE IT UP

Got an aluminum frame that's looking dirty and tired? Use a 3M Scotch-Brite pad (the green ones work, but the maroon ones #7447 are even better) and some WD-40 or similar lube to clean and buff the aluminum. Wipe off the aluminum oxide that results, then wash with soap and water and dry the aluminum afterward. Never use steel wool on aluminum. Another cleaner for aluminum frames and graphics is the Mr. Clean Magic Eraser. These white spongy blocks will remove black marks from graphics and plastic and shine up aluminum. Mineral spirits and WD-40 are very good for the black marks left by your boots.

Either a 3M Scotch-Brite pad or a Mr. Clean Magic Eraser will polish up an aluminum frame.

ADD A HUMP

Adding a hump to your seat keeps you planted under hard acceleration and also helps you stay in the proper forward attack position. You can purchase ready-made notched seats from various companies or you can make your own pretty simply. Here's how to do it:

- What you'll need: An electric staple gun with short ($1/4$-inch or so) staples, a small flat-blade screwdriver, and needle-nose pliers to remove old and misplaced new staples, a piece of handlebar pad foam or pipe insulation foam, a razor knife, and a helper. This is a good time to install a new seat cover.
- You can either remove all the staples and replace the seat cover (easiest), or only remove enough staples in the center section of the seat cover so you can work the piece of foam insulation into place.

- Cut the piece of foam so it's only $3/4$ to 1 inch thick and not as wide as the seat.
- Where to put the hump depends on the size of the rider, but typically the right spot is just a couple inches behind the center of the seat, toward the back—this typically is about 12 inches from the back of the seat. Try different positions, but if it's too far back it won't do you any good. If it forces you to sit forward on the bike, then it's probably in the right spot.
- Glue in place with contact cement or silicone seal. Let the glue dry before reinstalling the cover.

VINYL BLING: INSTALLING NEW BIKE GRAPHICS

Graphics are the main way you personalize your bike and available designs number in the hundreds, plus you can order a custom design of your own creation. Installing graphics is pretty simple, but there are some tricks you need to know:

- Fenders can stay in place, but all other plastic pieces getting new graphics should be removed.
- Tools you'll need include contact cleaner, a razor knife, a needle, spray-on glass cleaner, and a hair dryer. A plastic application squeegee with smooth edges (feel the edge to make sure it's smooth) comes in handy if you have one; otherwise use a credit card.
- Have a clean work area and nothing else on your schedule, as you'll need a dose of patience to do it right.
- Clean the plastic thoroughly. Really, really, really thoroughly. Start with soap and water, followed by contact cleaner or mineral spirits. Make sure there's no old glue residue on old plastic.
- If the plastic is heavily scratched, it's better to replace it with new pieces, although you can try to smooth the scratches with #600 fine wet/dry sandpaper. Never expect new graphics to hide the plastic's battle scars.
- Let the graphics warm up in the sun or in a warm room so they become flexible. Never install cold graphics on cold plastic or in a cold garage.
- Pick the one that's the simplest to install for your first victim. It'll give you some much-needed practice. A front number plate background is a good starting point.
- Do a dry run without removing the backing paper. See how it lines up and where you might have a fit problem.
- Now go wash your hands! Really wash them so there's no grease or dirt left.
- Some people install the graphics dry, while others use application fluids, such as glass cleaner, that allow the graphics to be repositioned. Both methods work.
- Spray some glass cleaner on the plastic and peel a portion of the backing paper off at one corner. The glass cleaner allows you to reposition the graphic. Some of the graphic companies offer their own application fluid which you might want to try.
- Hold most of the graphic up and away from the plastic while positioning the exposed portion. Once you have it aligned the way you want, start working the decal downward, starting in the middle and going side-to-side with your thumb or squeegee, using a sweeping motion. Work the bubbles out.
- Keep working it into place with your thumb while peeling off more of the backing. Always work each new section from the middle out to the edges.
- If you get a crease, it's okay to lift the decal up and reposition.
- Shroud graphics are usually easy so long as you get them positioned correctly around the mounting holes. Again, line things up in advance, take your time, use some glass cleaner to ease positioning, and work the bubbles out progressively with your thumbs and squeegee.
- The toughest graphics to install are the side number plate backgrounds because of all the curves in the plastic, especially the side with the pipe. Plenty of patience and some help from the hair dryer to make the decal more

A decal application kit can save you a lot of time and headaches.

What you'll need: squeegee (make sure the edges are smooth), glass cleaner, razor knife, pin to prick air bubbles, hair dryer, and two heaping loads of patience. The side panel on the exhaust side is usually the biggest challenge because of the curves. Use patience, heat, and glass cleaner. For some tight curves you may have to slit the graphic for a better fit.

flexible and help the graphics stretch around the curves is what you need.
- Don't overheat or overstretch the decal. Take it slow and get it right.
- Even with the patience of a saint and the steady hands of a brain surgeon, expect to have some fit problems and air bubbles. Use a needle to puncture air bubbles and work them flat. Where things don't line up the way you want, use the razor knife to fine tune things or cut the graphic so it fits over an especially tricky curve in the plastic.

GRIP TAPE

While you can buy special grip tapes that the skateboard crowd loves, your hardware store has high-traction tapes that are easy to cut to fit and install at a lower cost. Whatever grip tape you choose, clean the frame or plastic with contact cleaner before installing. Some grip tapes are very aggressive and will wear away your pants and boots at a high rate.

Cheap grip tape for your bike is as close as your hardware store.

Keep the plastic fantastic by applying a detailing product like Maxima SC1 after washing the bike. It reduces fading and restores the shine.

- If the decal is going on a gas tank, drain the tank. And to keep the fumes from bubbling a gas tank decal, don't park the bike in the sun (heat causes more fumes). If the bike is going to be unused for a while, drain it.
- Let new graphics sit for 24 hours before you go riding to ensure proper adhesion.

Another alternative is to let the pros do the work. DeCal Works, for one, will install the graphics for you on fresh new plastic.

Graphics Maintenance

Unlike diamonds, graphics aren't forever. They get worn, blasted by power washers, ripped in crashes, and scratched on muddy days when your pants grind the slop into them. Here are a few things you can do to make them last longer:

- Go easy with the power washer. Aiming a couple thousand psi of water at the edges of your graphics will cause them to lift up and start peeling.
- While the graphics are still fresh and clean, seal the edges to the plastic with some clear nail polish. It's a lot of work but worth it, since a set of graphics and custom backgrounds can set you back $150 or more.
- If edges do come loose, use contact cement to reattach. Clean any dirt stuck to the adhesive or edges. (If you've never used contact cement before, read the directions first.)
- Any graphic that goes on a plastic gas tank, unless it's perforated to let the gas fumes pass through, will eventually peel off. Even if perforated, over time the gas fumes that migrate through the plastic will discolor the graphics. Some bleach may get rid of the gas fume yellow, but there isn't any permanent fix.
- In high-wear areas, add a layer of clear vinyl over the graphics to help protect them.
- If your bike is approaching four years of age, start shopping for new graphics. Many makers stop offering graphics around that time, which explains why you see so many older bikes that have junky do-it-yourself logos or are completely bare of graphics.

KEEPING THE PLASTIC FANTASTIC

It's been decades since motocross bikes wore polished alloy tanks and fenders, and for good reason. Plastic doesn't dent, usually doesn't develop leaks, and it provides a lot of color options.

That still doesn't mean they last forever, so give some thought to the future when you'll be selling or trading in your bike. What I do is remove the stock plastic while it's still new, putting it away in a box, and then install aftermarket plastic with my new graphics before I ride the first time. This gives me a set of fresh OEM plastic with stock graphics to reinstall when it's time to sell it and a set of clean, scratch-free plastic for the new graphics without having to remove the original graphics, which can be an annoying, time-consuming, and sometimes impossible job.

Anodized billet aluminum pieces aren't just eye candy. Aftermarket chain adjusters have better, deeper reference marks and this one is reversible to easily accommodate different size sprockets without having to lengthen or shorten the chain.

Plastic can be welded or even glued together along cracks or "stitched" back together with small zip-ties. But all of that is a lot of work and you still have plastic that looks a little off. Replacement is better, although with older bikes, sometimes that's difficult or impossible. Maier Plastics (www.maier-mfg.com) is a good source for finding replacement pieces for older bikes. Scouring eBay sometimes works, too. If your bike is nearing—or past—the five year mark, it's smart to buy some spare plastic, especially shrouds (fender designs don't change that often). Get some graphics while you're at it, as after five years, replacement graphics are hard to come by.

Plastic requires some maintenance to keep from fading. Maxima SC1 and similar products restore the shine, ward off dirt and mud, and reduce fading. Use it after washing the bike.

BILLET PIECES

If your bike absolutely required an anodized billet aluminum piece, the manufacturers would likely be providing it in the first place. Billet bling may enhance durability but it's also mostly jewelry for your favorite motorcycle.

That's not a bad thing. As with custom graphics, if it helps make the bike look the way you want, and the price isn't a problem, then by all means add some billet touches.

There is one place where the billet replacements can make a difference, though: your wheels. Use the replacement rim lock covers to keep the rim lock threads from corroding and becoming hard to remove. Colorful billet tire valve caps make it easier to find the tire stem in a hurry.

Other useful bits of billet bling include sturdy chain guards near the countershaft, axle blocks with clearly marked marks, oil filler caps, and dipsticks, since the color will be a useful reminder to check the oil.

WHITE CREASES IN PLASTIC

Some colors of plastic develop white stress creases after a crash. You may be able to make the white disappear by using a heat gun to warm up the plastic. Guide it along the crease and see what happens. Take your time and the color should reappear.

Heating up plastic will often remove—or at least improve—a white crease from crash damage.

HOW TO WASH A BIKE WITHOUT A POWER WASHER

As effective as a power washer can be at removing mud and grime, that hard stream of water coming out of the nozzle can do a lot of damage, especially to seals, bearings, and graphics. There's a better, safer (for the bike) way:

Shout laundry spot cleaner makes a great, inexpensive bike wash. It floats off grime and grease and leaves the bike smelling good. And did I mention cheap? Buy it in quart bottles.

- What you need: a garden hose, Shout laundry cleaner (a big bottle is $5 or so), a nylon scrub brush, a car-washing sponge, towels, and if available, an air compressor with a blower gun nozzle.
- Put the bike up on the stand, plug the pipe and side panel air intakes (use tape), and then soak the bike down thoroughly with water from the hose. A lot of the mud will fall off at this point on its own.
- With the bike still wet, spray on Shout laundry cleaner. It cuts grease and grime like you won't believe, but you won't see the results right away. Shout is much less expensive than specialized motorcycle cleaners but it works just as well and leaves the bike smelling fresh and clean.
- After letting the Shout sit for a few minutes, use the hose again to clean off the bike. The Shout has great dirt- and grease-cutting power, yet it's safe on metals, plastics, and vinyl. For stubborn areas, hit it with the nylon brush or sponge.
- Repeat the wet bike/Shout/wait/rinse cycle again. Generally two or three wash cycles will clean off even the worst mud-crusted bike. It's a little more work than just pounding away with the power washer, but the bike gets just as clean (cleaner really) and you don't do any damage to bearings and seals.
- Once clean, wipe it off with the towel.
- Spray WD-40 or some other water-dispersing spray on the chain.
- Power up the air compressor and use it to blow out water trapped in nooks, the chain, the brake pads, and caliper pistons (the pistons are ferrous metal and can seize up), controls and so on. If you don't have an air compressor, start the bike up and ride it up the driveway a couple times.
- Apply a plastic detailing product such as Maxima SC1. Do this outside as the fumes can be overpowering. Then wipe it down.
- Stick a paper towel under the carb and loosen the drain bolt on the carb and let the fuel drain out, along with any water or debris that may be there. Turn on the fuel for just a few seconds to be sure the fuel line is flushed out.
- Lube the chain.

Chapter 7
Ground Power: Chains, Clutches, and Transmissions

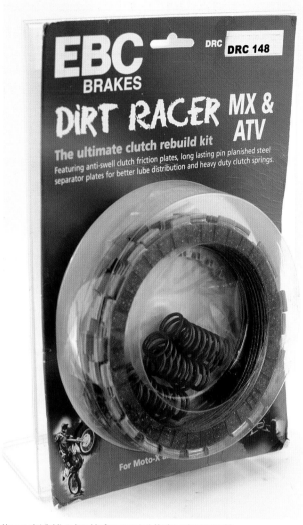

Have a clutch kit on hand before you start. You're going to need it.

Any time you have the clutch cover off, check the basket for notches. If you find any notches, the clutch basket will need replacing, sooner rather than later. Get an aftermarket replacement basket as they're much tougher than the OEM parts.

Sure, spending $2,000-plus on engine modifications and a full-race titanium-slash-carbon-fiber exhaust system is fun if your wallet has enough oomph, but all that expensive new horsepower has to find its way to the ground somehow. The drive train is what gets the job done. Your bike's tranny, clutch, and chain/sprocket require periodic attention and some low-buck upgrades to harness and deliver all that power. None of this is sexy, which is why they're usually at the bottom of the dirt biker's maintenance list. Here's what you need to know.

CLUTCH REPLACEMENT ESSENTIALS

Clutch jobs are easy and are a regular maintenance item for any rider. If the clutch has gotten grabby, sticky, notchy, or is slipping under power, it's time to check it out (see the sidebar "Is My Clutch Toast?" at right).

Step One: Before you do anything else, check the condition and routing of the clutch cable. Make sure the cable isn't twisted, bent, kinked, or pinched because it's been misrouted. Check your owner's manual for correct cable routing as it's easy to get it wrong. Make sure it's lubricated and moves smoothly—and if not, lube it so it does (see below). Kinked cables need to be replaced and the general consensus is that aftermarket cables are better than the factory stuff, but any new cable is better than an old abused one. If you have a hydraulic clutch, make sure the reservoir is full with fresh mineral fluid.

Step Two: Check the clutch lever and perch. If the clutch lever is floppy, bent, or binding, you need a new lever. When clutch levers wear out, so does your ability to smoothly feed out the clutch. Lubricate with an aerosol lube to keep it moving free and flush out any dirt that might be gunking things up. Replace a worn-out clutch lever.

Step Three: If you don't want to change the oil, lay the bike on its side, clutch cover facing up (don't do this if the gas tank is full). Remove the brake pedal so you have clear access to the cover (you may be able to get enough working room around the brake pedal by pushing the caliper's pistons in with a screwdriver). With the clutch cover off, take a close look at the clutch basket, checking for deep ridges. If the basket has ridges cut into it, every time you operate the clutch, the plates' tabs get hung up on the notches and you get a jerky clutch

CLUTCH CHANGE SHORTCUT

Gotta change the clutch plates? The manual will tell you to drain the oil and put it up on a stand and do this, do that, yada-yada. A shortcut—if you have fresh oil in the bike or no oil on hand (you're at the races)—is to lay the bike on its side, clutch cover facing up. No need to drain the oil. Just remove the clutch cover, do what you have to do, button it back up, and you're good to go.

action. The clutch basket fingers have to be smooth so the plates can move in and out smoothly. A basket that's lightly notched *may* be temporarily salvageable with some careful filing, but this is a temporary fix because the increased play will cause the basket to get notched again quicker and deeper. A notched clutch basket can't be repaired; a replacement is necessary and do not use the OEM part. Heavy-duty forged clutch baskets from Hinson, Wiseco, Barnett, and similar firms are much tougher than stock.

Step Four: Of course you were smart enough to plan ahead and order a good quality clutch kit from Barnett, EBC, or your dealer. A clutch kit will include new fiber and metal clutch plates plus clutch springs. Rather than bothering to see if the springs or plates are in spec, just replace everything. You may also need a new clutch cover gasket. When putting in the new plates, remember that a fiber plate is always the first plate to go on. New clutch plates need to be soaked in oil before installation. Only use dead dino (petroleum) oil in a clutch, never synthetic. Soak the plates by putting them in a baggie and pour in the oil or use the hard plastic packaging they come in. Let the plates soak for 24 to 48 hours. Don't skip this step as this impregnates the friction material, which helps stop initial wear and greatly prolongs clutch life.

Step Five: Remove the old clutch plates and springs, keeping everything in order as you take it out. Install the new plates in reverse order, followed by the pressure plate and the new springs. If all is well, button things up using a new clutch cover gasket, fill the transmission per specs, and you're good to go.

Soak the new plates in clean oil for 24 hours. Use a baggie or use the hard plastic packaging.

IS MY CLUTCH TOAST?

Here's how to understand what your clutch is telling you. To see if it's slipping, do this:

- Riding in a safe, flat area, put the bike in second gear and travel at a steady speed, say 20 to 30 mph. Now give it a handful of throttle and pay attention to how the bike responds. Do the RPMs jump, but there's little or no actual acceleration? Then the fiber plates are worn down and need to be replaced along with the clutch springs.
- If clutch action is notchy and chatters or the bike won't easily shift into neutral, the clutch basket is notched and will need replacement.
- Note that a worn out or stretched clutch cable can also cause slipping.
- When you drain the transmission oil, if it smells burnt, your clutch is toast. You may be able to smell it without even seeing the oil.
- With the clutch cover off, if the fiber plates are glazed, they're toast no matter how much fiber is still on them.
- If the metal plates are blued, they're junk. If the clutch chatters, yet the clutch basket isn't notched, it may be a warped steel plate. The metal plate may be flat when cold, but warps when heated (any time it's in use).
- The manual tells you to measure the clutch plates to see if they're still good, but realistically, if you have the clutch cover off anyway, it makes more sense to replace everything (all plates, springs) with a new clutch kit. If you're a hard-core racer, you should be doing this on a regular basis.
- Steel or aluminum drive plates? Aluminum plates are easier on the inner clutch hub and are lighter, producing a quicker, rev-happy feel. However, aluminum doesn't last nearly as long as steel and dumps aluminum sludge into the oil. A compromise between the durability of steel and aluminum's free-spinning response are Akadized aluminum plates. These are not available for all models and aren't cheap (about $100 for the Akadized drive plates only).
- Clutches heat up and expand with use. Adjust lever play only when the engine is cool. Free-play at the lever should be about $3/16$ of an inch (4.7mm)—raid your pocket for some change because that's a hair less than three quarters.

Pocket change: Three quarters are just a hair over what your free-play should be.

GEAR RATIO MATH

You can easily calculate the gear ratio by dividing the number of teeth on the countershaft sprocket into the teeth on the rear sprocket. For example, if the numbers are 13 and 50, then the gear ratio is 3.84. But what does that mean in a practical let's-go-racing sense?

- As the gear ratio number gets higher, the gearing is lower (you're gearing down). This makes it better for hills, motocross, turns, and tight trails. You shift more often, but you're in the meaty portion of the powerband most of the time.
- As the gear ratio number gets lower, the gear ratio is higher (you're gearing up). This makes the bike more suited for high speed work, desert racing, and extremely fast courses with few turns.

GEARING CHEAT SHEETZ®

Confused as to whether to gear up, down, or sideways? Use this chart and these rules of thumb:

- To determine your bike's gear ratio, divide the smaller number (countershaft sprocket) into the bigger number (rear sprocket teeth). Thus a 13/48 gives you a 3.69 gear ratio.
- Gearing UP means LESS teeth on the rear and a higher top speed.
- Gearing DOWN means ADDING teeth to the rear and a lower top speed but quicker response in each gear.
- Adding a tooth to the countershaft is the same as adding 3½ teeth to the rear.
- For full-size bikes, the smallest countershaft you can usually run is 13T and the largest is 15T.

Front/Rear	12	13	14	15
45	3.75	3.46	3.21	3.00
46	3.83	3.53	3.28	3.06
47	3.91	3.61	3.35	3.13
48	4.00	3.69	3.42	3.20
49	4.08	3.76	3.50	3.26
50	4.16	3.84	3.57	3.33
51	4.25	3.92	3.64	3.40
52	4.33	4.00	3.71	3.46
53	4.41	4.07	3.78	3.53

A gearing calculator is nice to have, but any calculator will work fine. It's just basic math.

THE CHAIN GANG

Riders think of chains as low-tech, but there are around 500 individual parts in a typical chain and it only takes one of these to fail to give you problems. Keeping the chain happy is simple enough, but there are some tricks and tips you should know:

Tension Headaches: Chain Adjustment the Right Way

- The bike has to be on a stand, period. Get the rear wheel off the ground somehow.
- Loosen the axle nut but keep it moderately snug.
- Now loosen the chain adjuster nuts. By keeping the axle nut snug, the axle blocks stay in alignment and you can use the adjuster bolts to wind the axle blocks back like a jack.
- If the axle blocks have hard-to-read alignment notches, either put some paint in the notch marks to make them easier to see or get aftermarket axle blocks that have highly visible marks. Zip-Ty Racing makes one of the best versions of these.
- Never assume that the marks on the axle blocks are correct. There are ways and tools to measure whether or not the chain is tracking straight on the sprockets, but you can check it by spinning the rear wheel while sighting down the chain and seeing (and listening) if the chain is tracking straight. The chain should spin freely and straight—any side-to-side movement means it's not aligned, no matter what the axle block marks claim. If it's way off, it'll be making a clackity noise.
- How much slack? Your manual has a number in there someplace, but the rule of thumb is "two fingers" (not three) between the chain and the chain pad on the top of the swingarm, which is about halfway between the sprockets. Spin the wheel a little and check the slack again. It's always better to have the chain a little loose rather than too tight—the key words being "a little."
- Measure chain slack with the bike ON the stand unless your manual says otherwise (a few do).
- A chain that is too loose (too much slack) causes premature wear to both chain and sprockets, increasing the chance of a thrown or snapped chain which will wad up and smash the engine cases—an expensive fix you definitely want to avoid.
- A chain that's too tight will quickly wear out countershaft sprocket bearings and seals and negatively affects rear suspension action.
- Whenever you adjust the tension or reinstall the rear wheel, place a rag or a wrench on the sprocket and rotate the wheel until it's jammed tightly in place. This forces the wheel forward, moving the chain adjusters forward against the swingarm so you can tighten them down.

What Chain? What Sprockets?

First of all, chains and sprockets are commodity items, so don't agonize about wearing them out and using them up—that's their role. They get used up and thrown away, just like engine oil, tires, and other high-wear items. Since they're commodities, you can save a few dollars by using no-name brands instead of the heavily advertised stuff. Generally, the no-name versions are just as good and a lot cheaper.

- Dirt bike chains come in two versions: standard roller and O-ring/X-ring. Both of the "ring" versions use tiny rubber rings to keep grease in place. This keeps the rollers constantly lubricated, so the chain is slower to stretch and you'll go further between adjustments. An X-ring chain is a variation on the O-ring version, except with a twisted X-shaped sealing ring design that's claimed to hold in grease better and is narrower.
- Ring-style chains are the preferred choice of enduro/cross-country riders. Because they're wider (those rings take up space), some bikes require a spacer to keep the sprockets in alignment. The knock on ring-style chains is that they're more expensive and usually heavier than other chains. The extra mass is why most motocross riders don't use them. The slightly greater weight affects acceleration and throttle response—although you'll probably have a hard time noticing the difference if you're riding a 450cc bike.

Before you tighten up the chain adjusters, put a rag on the rear sprocket and spin the wheel so the rag is jammed between the chain and rear sprocket. This moves the rear wheel up against the adjusters so they can be tightened.

Stainless-steel sprockets are so durable they may outlast the bike.

Standard, O-ring, and X-ring chains. You can see the difference in thickness.

If your sprocket teeth are hooked like this, the sprocket is long past the junk stage. Those teeth will instantly chew up a new chain if you keep on using the sprocket.

- Summarized, an O- or X-ring chain is going to weigh more, cost more, and may require a spacer, but should last longer and need far fewer adjustments.
- Countershaft sprockets are a commodity item. They will always be steel and there's little or no difference between them as long as they fit properly.
- Some countershaft sprockets are designed to be installed with one side facing out for standard chains and the other side facing out if using a wider O-ring chain.
- Rear sprockets come in lots of flavors and colors: solid steel, steel with lots of lightening holes, aluminum, bi- or tri-metal assemblies, and stainless steel. That's also how the prices break down, with solid steel the cheapest and bi-metal or stainless the high-buck choice but usually the longest lasting. The actual weight difference between

the different metal types is relatively minor, but can't be totally ignored—you pay more for less metal, tougher metal, and more holes. For motocross, a lightweight aluminum sprocket is the preferred choice, as the lighter weight adds to acceleration and throttle response.
- Color does not add any speed, sorry.
- For enduro, cross-country, and play riding where mud and deep sand are common, choose a lightweight steel sprocket paired with an O-ring chain, and the combo will last a decent time with minimal need for chain adjustment.
- Any sprocket you choose should have "mud grooves"— the scalloped cuts between each tooth. These grooves give mud a place to go as it's squeezed between the chain and sprocket.
- If most of your riding is in mud or sand, get a steel rear as it will significantly outlast aluminum.
- Steel is also the way to go if you're on a tight budget as it'll last three to five times longer than aluminum.
- Stainless-steel and tri-metal sprocket designs are very good, very durable, and very expensive compared to the others. If the price doesn't bother you or you simply want the best, definitely get one. These sprockets will usually outlast the chains and maybe the whole bike.
- As to whether to go with a brand name or not, it's more personal choice and what your budget can handle than anything else. Sprockets and chains are commodities that get used up and thrown away. Don't expect them to become family heirlooms.

Run New with New

Whenever you replace a worn-out chain, also replace both sprockets. Always run new with new. Putting a new chain on worn sprockets or vice-versa just makes everything wear out that much quicker—30 to 40 percent quicker by some tests. The exception to this would be if you'd recently replaced sprockets or the old chain was relatively new. Buy good chains, whether name brand or not, but remember that this is a high-wear part that needs regular replacement. Buy a chain that's tough enough for the stresses you're going to throw its way because using a lower-grade chain is a false economy if it breaks during a race or strands you out in the boonies. Riding a lot of sandy or muddy races will wear out the chain and sprockets that much quicker.

SILICONE THE CLIP

Factory mechanics do this and so can you. On a clean chain, after the circlip is installed, seal the entire contact area around the circlip with silicone seal. This keeps the circlip from vibrating and stops grit from working its way in and grinding away at things. Some teams also seal the splined countershaft sprocket for the same reason.

What Lube Where?

The facts of life concerning lubricating chains, what lubes to use, how to know what you need:

- There's no point in lubricating a dirty chain. All you're doing is lubricating the dirt, which makes it attract even more dirt.
- Clean your chain with a stiff brush, preferably one intended for chains. Get as much of the crud off as possible. Do NOT use a power washer unless you want to significantly shorten the chain's life. A high pressure washer forces water into the chain rollers, leading to premature rust and can even blow out the lube from an O-ring.
- Don't use a wire bristle brush on an O-ring chain. It'll damage the rubber rings.
- With the chain clean, warm the chain up before applying lube. A lap or two will get it warm enough to ensure good penetration by the lube into the chain rollers. Lube the side of the chain that actually contacts the sprockets—the inside of the chain, not the top.
- Thick tacky chain lubes are only for perfectly dry conditions because they're so sticky that dirt sticks to the chain. That dirt turns into grinding compound that eats away your chain and sprockets.
- Ride nothing but sand? Then use a silicone spray like Maxima SC1. It's not a chain lube, but it does coat the links. And when allowed to dry, it actually repels sand and dust.
- Use chain wax or a clear and lightweight lube in just about all other conditions. The waxy nature of this stuff repels water and dirt, and is best used in wet conditions—in other words, the typical watered-and-groomed motocross track.
- Once lubed, adjust the chain to specs.

Seized Chain Adjuster

Few things are more frustrating than trying to adjust the chain and discovering that either the butter-soft locking nut has rounded over or the adjuster itself is seized in place on the swingarm. Here's what to do:

- Any time you notice the locking nut starting to round, take the time to pull the wheel, remove the adjuster, and thread on a new lock nut. Before reinstalling the adjuster bolt, coat the threads with anti-seize compound. Trust me, you'll be glad you did.
- If the adjuster bolt is seized tight, try a heat gun first. Heat up the end of the swingarm. That might be enough to loosen it, but if not, hit it with some Loctite Freeze & Release. The cold shocks the corrosion so that penetrating oil can get in and go to work.
- Still stuck? See if there's a drain hole at the bottom of your swingarm so you can spray some penetrating lube inside. No drain hole? Drill one.

Bet you didn't know there are chain lubes for different situations. Chain wax is the most versatile and best suited for motocross.

Clean your chain before applying chain lube, otherwise you're just lubricating the dirt.

- If the adjuster bolt is frozen solid or breaks off, you have some work ahead of you. Use an EZ-Out to remove the broken bit or pull the swingarm and take it to a machine shop or your dealer to have the broken piece removed, as it can be a bear to get out and it's easy to make things worse if you don't know what you're doing.
- If the threads inside the swingarm are messed up, you'll have to install a thread insert or use a Swingarm Buddy (www.protekk.com). This is a $35 repair kit that includes everything you need to fix a broken chain adjuster bolt. You need one per adjuster.

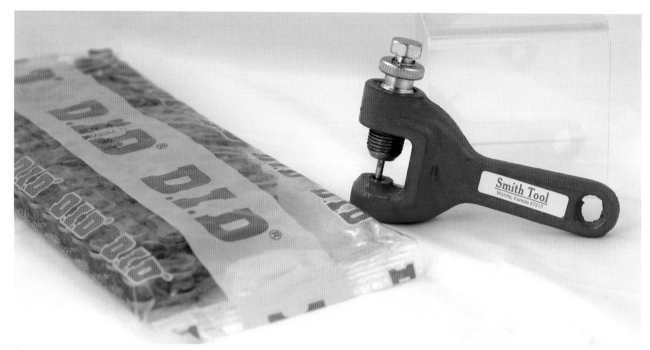

Breaking a chain is a simple task if you have the right tools. Use a full-size chain breaker ($20 or so) and press the pin out of a link by tightening the handle. You can also use a grinder to remove the pin heads, followed with a little bit of help from a punch.

Chain adjusters break and the nuts tend to get rounded off. Replace them periodically.

HOW TO SHIFT

It seems simple, but there's more to shifting than just toeing the lever. The two things to understand: the *power curve* is the whole range of power from the engine; the *powerband* is that portion of the power curve where the engine's power delivery is strongest. What you want to understand and do:

- Shift *BEFORE* you hit the top of the power curve. If the engine is screaming at the top of its power curve, you're not going to go any faster until you shift and you've already missed the sweet spot.
- Shift while *IN* the powerband. This is where acceleration is at its best and you can feel the difference. You're aiming for the mid- to top portion of the power curve. This is the motor's meaty section, so learn how it feels (sound, vibration) when you're in and out of the powerband.
- Try to shift when the rear wheel isn't driving hard on the ground, such as in the air off a jump or when it's kicked up by a bump. This makes the shift easier and puts less stress on the gearbox, which helps reduce missed shifts.
- First gear is for use in the pits, rarely or never on the track.
- Power shift. This means holding the throttle on while flicking the clutch lever with a finger or two, but not completely engaging the clutch. A variation of this is to back off the throttle just a notch then toe the shifter. If you're pulling in the clutch completely before each shift, you're losing time on the track.
- Every shift costs you time. Carry the highest gear into a turn that still keeps you in the powerband coming out.

- Fallen a bit out of the powerband? Fan (slip) the clutch instead of downshifting. This gets the engine back into the powerband.
- Have your shifter in the right place and modify or replace it with an aftermarket unit so it fits you. A longer shifter with a larger tip is for someone with big feet, for example. Position the shifter so the tip is in line or slightly above the top of the footpegs. Pivoting footpegs make it easier to get your boot under the shifter tip and are a great fix if you're missing a lot of shifts.

GUIDE TO BEING A GEARHEAD

Want to be a lot faster? Then bone up on gearing basics and you'll see why this is the first thing you should look to when trying to improve the bike. Gearing (call it "final drive" if you want to sound techy) determines how fast you can go and how hard you have to work to get to that speed.

As delivered from the factory, your bike's gearing is a compromise. One of those compromises is the stock gearing which is usually geared too high to produce a middle-of-the-road response that allows the bike to work adequately for a wide variety of riders with different abilities. For the cut-and-thrust of racing, this isn't a compromise you'll be happy with.

When you next have the rear wheel off, unthread the chain adjusters completely from the swingarm. Clean the threads and then brush some anti-seize on before reinstalling them in the swingarm.

Position the shifter so it's level or slightly above the top of the footpeg. Buy (or modify) longer/shorter shift levers to make it fit your feet.

Sprocket bolts take a beating. Replace them when you install a new sprocket.

With three sprockets—one countershaft and two rears—you can adjust your gearing to just about any off-road riding situation you're likely to encounter.

One of the easiest and most effective performance modifications you can make is to tailor the gearing to match your riding abilities and the tracks or trails you ride most often. The scoop:

- Gearing determines two things: (1) the **rate** of acceleration—how fast you get up to speed—and (2) **top speed**. These are not the same things.
- Gearing changes can affect the bike's handling. When you change to a smaller rear sprocket without also changing the chain length, you're also moving the rear axle backwards, increasing the overall wheelbase. This is good for high-speed stability but not so good for turning. The opposite effect (shorter wheelbase, sharper turning) occurs when installing a larger rear sprocket. You may need to add/subtract chain links, raise or lower the forks, or make other adjustments to your suspension.
- You don't need a lot of different sprockets. Three sprockets are probably all you need. Take along a one-tooth smaller countershaft and one- and two-teeth larger rears. Those will give you everything you need for different tracks and conditions.
- Gear for what you need and what conditions you're riding in. For motocross, you want maximum acceleration in each gear—a punchy, responsive powerband that you can count on to help you clear jumps coming out of corners, rather than one aimed at maximum top speed. For motocross, an a full-sized bike your gearing combinations will typically be a 12-, 13-, or 14T C/S (countershaft) and 49- to 53T rear sprocket.
- Usually you will only make a one- or two-tooth change in gearing at a time.
- For enduro/cross-country work, you gear for higher top speed, with a more leisurely and broader power delivery in each gear. Here, the range of choices is usually 13- or 14T C/S and 46- to 50T rear.

- Don't limit yourself to rear sprockets only. Use the countershaft sprocket size to play with the ratios and keep the rear axle where you want it to be.
- At high altitude, engines produce less power and generally need to be geared down (more teeth on the rear).
- Avoid running the smallest possible countershaft sprocket; it's much harder on the chain.
- What works best? Experiment and find out. Unlike other performance changes that require big doses of time, money, and mechanical aptitude, gearing changes can be made quickly and a range of sprockets can be added to your toolbox for around $100 or less.
- Buy spare rear sprocket bolts. It's cheap insurance any time you start changing rear sprockets. Sprocket bolts take a helluva beating and should be checked and replaced often.
- Most modern sprocket bolts have Allen heads on one side. When tightening/loosening, use the Allen wrench to anchor the bolt head so it doesn't spin, but do your actual work on the lock nut. Never try and tighten things using the Allen head—you'll just mess it up.

THE NOT-SO-LITTLE STUFF

Chain guides, chain rollers, and chain sliders are all part of the big picture and all too often ignored.

- If you bend a chain guide—or even if you don't—replace it with a sturdier aftermarket unit. Most OEM versions crumble up too easily. Not only will it help keep the chain rolling straight, but it'll roll smoother because of better polyurethane rollers and be better able to shrug off rocks, branches, and other trail debris. Check out T.M. Designworks for the best chain sliders and chain guides.
- The chain slider on top of your swingarm not only protects the swingarm but also helps feed it to the countershaft. Keep an eye on wear so that you don't suddenly have the chain sawing into that expensive aluminum.
- Chain rollers (upper and lower) need to spin freely if they're going to do their job. Aftermarket versions have better bearings and tougher, better polyurethane rollers. Periodically take each of the rollers off; clean and grease or replace as necessary.
- Having a chain break is bad enough. Having it destroy the engine cases when it comes off is an expensive disaster. The stock plastic chain guards do nothing. Install a billet or heavy polyurethane case saver (a.k.a. case guard). These units protect the case if the chain breaks by keeping it from wadding up.

Install a rigid case saver to provide some protection from a broken chain wadding up and breaking those expensive engine cases.

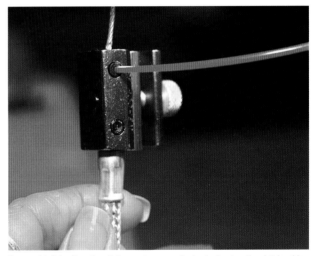

Buy a cable luber for a few dollars and on a regular basis shoot up the clutch cable to eliminate drag.

CABLE LUBING

A notchy clutch action may be coming from the clutch cable. If it's dry, it'll drag and release slowly or sometimes just freeze up. Once a month, lubricate the cables with a cable luber—it's the easy and effective way to tackle this little chore. For clutch cables, you only have to release the cable at the lever. For throttle cables you need to detach the cable from the carb so any grit inside the cable doesn't get flushed down into the carb where it can hang things up.

While you're at it, clean out all the controls with some blasts of brake cleaner, check for wear and excess play, and then lubricate the lever pivots with WD-40 or similar products. You want your clutch working smoothly, with proper play, so it releases with a snap when the gate drops. If the levers are flopping around in the pivot because they're worn, replace either the lever blade or the entire assembly. You want these controls to be s-m-o-o-t-h operators.

CHAIN PLATE CLAMP

Sometimes when you're replacing a chain, especially O-ring types, you can't seem to get the plate on deep enough to slide the master clip into place. Take a C-clamp and a nut large enough to fit over the chain pin and tighten it up. The plate will snap into place.

Chapter 8
Mix It Up: Understanding Dirt Bike Carbs, Jetting, Filters, and Fuel

For all its mechanical complexity, a motorcycle engine is really pretty simple in operation, needing only four things to run: fuel, air, compression, and ignition. This chapter deals with the first two components and how they come together.

Carburetors are still the predominant fuel mixing device, and even with electronic fuel injection (EFI) now common in cars and street bikes, the majority of dirt bikes will still rely on a carb for many years to come. There's a lot of science,

engineering, theory and hard-earned practical experience behind that fuel-air mixing device that your right wrist controls.

But you don't really care about all the science and engineering, nor have any desire to wade through a thick book on the topic. You just want your bike to start easily and always run the way it should. Accomplishing that means understanding what your carb is doing and how to tell when the jetting needs attention.

Modern thumpers bury the carb inside the frame rails with no consideration for rider access. Take off the subframe to get at the carb. You don't have to completely unbolt the subframe; just loosen the fasteners and swing it down.

In this chapter I'll walk you through the basics of jetting, simple but useful modifications, fuel, and related topics.

THE JETTING COMPROMISE

Like everything else about your bike, as delivered from the factory the carburetion is a compromise. Typically, the manual will tell you that they're jetted for sea level and the hot, low-humidity conditions of Southern California. Live any place where conditions are different and you need to rejet. Even if you do live in SoCal, you'll be doing some rejetting to compensate for modifications such as a different pipe, race fuel, or any of a number of other factors.

The carb's fussiness and complexity are why electronic fuel injection (EFI) is now moving into the motocross world with the golden promise of always being jetted perfectly to match the conditions. Of course EFI will just lead to another set of tuning variables you'll have to learn.

GETTING TO THE CARB

In motorcycling's not too distant past, carburetors were simple devices: They were easy to see and working on them was a

matter of loosening a couple of clamps. You could change the main jet or needle clip position in a couple of minutes. This is still the case on most two-strokes, but with most of the thumpers, well . . ..

Today's four-stroke motors sit in shrink-wrapped perimeter frames with the carb tucked snugly inside. The simple solution for gaining access to the carb is to remove everything that's in the way: the seat, side panels, subframe, and possibly the tank and rear shock. As always, check your manual for advice and what order to do things because the guys who put it together are also the ones who can best tell you how to take it apart.

Dirt is the enemy of carbs, so before you unbolt anything, get the bike as clean as you can and then continue to keep it clean as you take it apart. It's always best to do things in the garage with a lot of light to help, but if you're doing this in the pits, at least spread out a clean shop rag for the parts to rest on.

KEIHIN FCR MODIFICATIONS

If you ride a four-stroke bike, you have a Keihin FCR carb. It's a good carb but not perfect (what is?), so improving its

The R&D Racing Power Bowl fixes most of what's wrong with a Keihin FCR and you can do it all yourself in an hour. Cost is $250 and worth every cent.

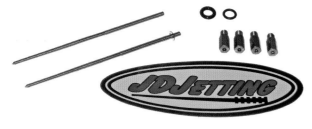

A JD Jetting kit is tailored for your area, altitude, and bike and comes with complete instructions. Install their jets and you're good to go.

performance and correcting some of its faults has become a cottage industry. Here's what to do, in what order, and what it costs:

- The R&D Racing Power Bowl requires a $250 investment but delivers easier starting, instant throttle response, reduces hot engine stalling, improves low-end performance, and eliminates the hesitation and bogging that FCRs are prone to. It's a bolt-on product that replaces the stock float bowl and the benefits are so obvious that the initially steep price will seem like a bargain.

You need an aftermarket fuel screw (also called a mixture screw) that extends far enough so you can reach it easily. An R&D Racing Flex Jet ($32) makes it even more convenient.

- If the R&D Power Bowl is too much and all you want to do is get rid of the bog that comes when landing from a jump, then install a Boyesen QuickShot accelerator pump cover. For $90, it's a quick and simple fix.
- Why agonize over what the jetting should be, when someone else has figured it out already? That's the idea behind installing a JD Jetting kit or similar precision jetting kit developed via dyno testing. A JD Jetting kit is tailored to fit your bike, locale, and modifications. The typical kit provides two needles, several main jets, clips, and good instructions. Cost is about $75 at www.jdjetting.com.
- You need a fuel screw (also called the mixture screw). Your FCR carb has a tiny inaccessible fuel screw buried on the bottom of the carb. Being able to adjust the fuel screw quickly without tools is vital for smooth throttle response, especially as the weather changes. Lots of companies make fuel screws, so you'll pay around $20. Just don't lose the tiny O-ring when installing. The ultimate version is the R&D Racing Flex Jet, which provides even easier access and holds its settings.
- Let somebody else do it. Carb mods can be done by a pro shop such as Zip-Ty Racing. You ship your carb to them with the particulars of your riding area, and they tune and perform some changes that make it work the way it should. Expect to pay about $100 plus shipping.
- A Boyesen Power X-Wing inserted into the carb boot straightens out the turbulent airflow, increasing velocity and improving throttle response. This is not a must-do for anyone, although the hard-core racer will appreciate the improved responsiveness. Cost is about $125.

JETTING BASICS 101

You don't have to become an expert at jetting in order to have your bike properly jetted. It simply requires a bit of knowledge about how the carb converts the action in your right wrist into forward motion. This is the cram course in Jetting 101.

- It may not be the jetting. Before you start tearing into the carb, make sure the air filter is clean, valve clearances are correct, fresh fuel is in the tank, the throttle grip isn't slipping, the throttle cables aren't sticky, the engine isn't worn out (piston/rings, low compression), the muffler or header pipe aren't crushed, and that the brakes aren't sticking.
- One last thing to eliminate is float height. Make sure it's correct. A too-lean or too-rich idle speed is a sign the float height may be off. With the carb off and float bowl removed, hold it at a 45-degree angle so the floats are barely touching the stops. Measure

Mikuwi TMX carburetor

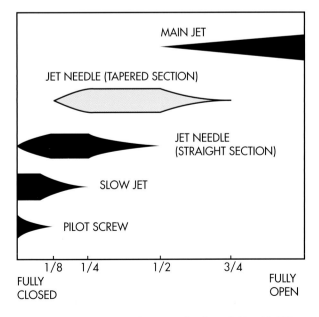

These four are the jets you need to focus on: needle, pilot, main jet, and for FCR-equipped thumpers, the fuel screw.

the distance (a proper float gauge is best, but you can use a good ruler in a pinch) against what your manual says it should be. Adjust float level by gently bending the little float tab with a small screwdriver.

- Know what the carb is telling you. See the next section on jetting symptoms.
- Although there are multiple jet circuits in a carb, you really only have to focus on four (three if it's a two-stroke): main jet, needle jet, pilot jet, and for four-strokes, the fuel screw.
- Jet function depends on throttle position. The chart on page 93 identifies what jets are working at what point.
- When changing jet sizes, only go up or down one jet size at a time.

Pilot (Slow) Jet Basics: Quarter-throttle

The pilot jet (also called the slow jet) controls the mixture up to a quarter-throttle and is the easiest to nail down. If your bike is "poppy" off the bottom or hard to start, both are symptoms of a too-lean pilot. Dialing it in:

- If you have a thumper with an FCR carb and fuel screw, see the section on using the fuel screw. It tells you whether or not your pilot jet is correct.
- Summed up, if the best setting for your fuel screw is about $1^1/_2$ to $2^1/_2$ turns out depending on conditions, your pilot jet is correct.
- The higher the pilot jet number, the richer the jet.
- The pilot jet is inside the float bowl.

Needle Jet Basics: Quarter to Three-Quarter Throttle

The needle controls the mixture from quarter- to three-quarter throttle—essentially the whole mid-range. The needle has more effect on jetting than all the others put together but is typically the jet most often ignored. Dialing it in:

- Get the pilot jet and the main jet dialed in before worrying about the needle as otherwise you will be wasting your time.
- There's a lot of tuning range built into the needle, simply by moving the clip up or down on the notches. Use it!
- Needle clip position is always counted from the top down, with the first notch being number one.
- If you have the needle at either the very top or bottom clip positions, you need to go with a different needle. Your owner's manual will list the stock needle and optional sizes. As with any jetting change, if you need a different needle, go only one size up or down at a time.
- If you're serious about tuning your carb, buy some spare parts, especially needle clips, since they're so frustratingly easy to lose.

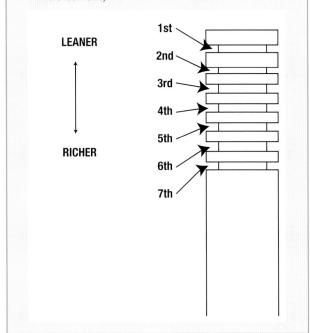

LINGO CHECK

- Raising the clip = leaner (the clip is put on a higher notch, so now the needle is deeper into the jet and less fuel can get out).
- Raising the needle = richer (the clip is put on a lower notch, so now the needle isn't as deeply into the jet and more fuel flows).

LEANER

RICHER

1st
2nd
3rd
4th
5th
6th
7th

Main Jet Basics: Three-quarter to WFO

It's usually pretty easy to identify main jet problems, as the bike simply has no guts at three-quarter throttle and above, and it feels like it's running out of gas. (It is!) In the worst case scenario, the main jet is so lean when the engine is at full throttle or working hard, that it leads to an engine failure. Dialing it in:

- Symptoms of a too-lean main jet are cutting out or popping from half- to full-throttle.
- Symptoms of a too-rich main jet are smoking and a stuffy feeling as the motor tries to clean out.
- To test the main jet, you need a long, flat area to ride so you can get deep into the throttle. Ride a gear higher than normal in order to put an extra load on the engine, which will highlight any main jet size problems.
- A correctly sized main jet will offer no hesitation when the throttle is cracked wide open from half-throttle. It should pull cleanly and crisply right up to the rev-limiter.
- In general, riders focus too much on the main jet and not enough on the needle.
- Main jet numbers are like the rest—the higher the number, the richer the jet.

JETTING CHEAT SHEETZ®

CARBURETOR OR PARTS		
	Moving the clip DOWN the jet needle makes it richer.	
	The jet needle and its clip positions affect the carb's mid-range from 1/4 to 3/4 throttle	
Main Jet:	The higher the number, the richer the main jet.	
	The main jet affects the carb's top-end from half to full open throttle.	
Air Screw:	Turning the air screw IN makes it leaner; OUT makes it richer.	
	The air screw affects carb's idle to quarter-throttle range.	
ENGINE CLUES		
Lean Engine Signs	Poor acceleration	
	Engine excessively hot or seizes	
	Detonation and pinging	
	Engine runs better when choke is applied	
	Spark plug is white	
Rich Engine Signs	Engine smokes heavily	
	Worsens as it warms up	
	Sluggish response throttle	
	Engine sounds dull and off-song	
	Applying the choke makes it worse	
	Spark plug is oily or fouls easily	
WEATHER AND ALTITUDE		
Jetting and Weather	Assumes your engine is jetted correctly for your altitude and normal (typical) conditions.	
It Gets Colder	Engine runs leaner; Richen jetting	
It Gets Warmer	Engine runs richer; Lean out jetting	
Humidity Drops	Engine runs leaner; Richen jetting	
Humidity Increases	Engine runs richer; Lean out jetting	
Higher Altitude	Engine runs richer; Lean out jetting	
Hot, Dry, and Sandy	Engine works harder; go richer	

MIX IT UP: UNDERSTANDING DIRT BIKE CARBS, JETTING, FILTERS, AND FUEL

FUEL SCREW BASICS:
DOWN LOW AND ALL OVER (THUMPERS ONLY)

Every Keihin FCR has a separate low-speed fuel system built in, controlled by the fuel screw (also called the mixture screw). If not adjusted properly, the bike will run rough and stumble noticeably. Here's how to deal with it:

- Install an aftermarket fuel screw that you can reach with your fingers (the stocker is buried at the bottom of the carb). See the next section for how to do this correctly. An alternative is the new R&D Racing Remote Flexjet fuel screw which is much more convenient to use and costs only about $30.
- Even though the fuel screw covers only the low engine speed range, if the fuel screw is not properly adjusted, it will affect the jetting across the whole throttle range.
- Turning a fuel screw IN leans the mixture. As the day gets hotter, you may need to turn the fuel screw in to lean things out.

- Turning a fuel screw OUT richens the mixture. When it's cool in the morning, turn the fuel screw out a notch to enrich the mixture.
- You adjust the fuel screw in quarter- or half-turns.
- To adjust the fuel screw, first warm up the engine and then bring it up to a fast idle of about 1,800 rpm. Now slowly tighten (turn in) the fuel screw until engine speed drops and nearly dies. Now turn it back out again until the engine runs clean and fast.
- Reset the idle speed down to low or no idle position and ride the bike. If it bogs, coughs, or stumbles, adjust it again until the bogging goes away. It's a trial-and-error process until you get used to how it should feel.
- Heat and humidity will change during the day, so change the fuel screw settings to match. Typically that means richer in the cool morning air, leaner when it warms up.
- The range of adjustment is small and the fuel screw will typically only be best between one and two-and-a-half turns out. If it needs more than three turns out to fix things, the pilot jet may be too small. If it takes less than one-half turn out to run well, then the pilot jet is too rich.

WHAT THE MOTOR IS TELLING YOU

Symptom	Possible Cause	Notes
Motor doesn't pull down low	Too rich	
Motor doesn't pull at top	Too lean	Go bigger on main jet
Poor throttle response	Too rich	
Great throttle response	Too lean	Two-strokes only
Popping through intake	Too lean	
Popping in exhaust	Too lean and/or air leak	Check the pipe connections
Hard starting	Can be either condition	
Constant misfiring	Too rich	
Irregular misfiring	Too lean	
Wet and oily plug	Too rich	Two-strokes only
White plug	Too lean	
Hesitation	Too lean	
Hole in the piston	Waayyy too lean	

INSTALLING AN ADJUSTABLE FUEL SCREW

The factory buries this important mixture adjustment screw at the bottom of the carb, but fortunately the aftermarket has ways to make it easy to access. Here's the routine:

- This is a must-do fix for all thumpers if you want a smooth-running engine. This little screw is that important.
- You may be able to do this with the carb rotated out for access to the bottom, but in most cases you're better off removing the Keihin so you can easily get at the tiny parts you'll be dealing with.
- Spread a clean shop rag underneath the Keihin to catch any parts that fall.
- With a flat-blade screwdriver, unscrew the fuel screw—it's the little screw at the bottom of the carb.
- There are (or should be) four pieces: the brass fuel screw, a spring, a flat washer, and a black O-ring. In most cases you will use the spring, washer, and O-ring with the aftermarket fuel screw.
- The tiny O-ring has a habit of getting stuck inside. Get it out with the spring or a small pick tool.
- Put the parts on the aftermarket fuel screw in this order: spring, washer, O-ring. Now thread it in the carb—it takes about eight turns to seat.
- Back it out one-and-a-half turns and bolt everything back up.
- With everything back in place, start the bike up and run it until it's warm. Turning the fuel screw in quarter-turns in each direction, experiment with throttle response until it feels crisp and clean.

NO MORE GUESSING

To take the guesswork out of carb jetting, use some White-Out, a silver-colored Sharpie, or similar marker to mark 1/8-inch reference marks on your throttle housing. Then make an index mark on your throttle grip with the throttle closed. Different jets come into play at different throttle settings. When you're trying to evaluate the jetting, you can now tell with a quick glance what part of the carburetion is running poorly at what throttle setting, rather than having to guess at the throttle position.

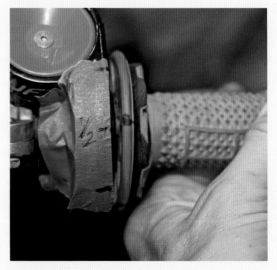

Know exactly what part of the throttle you're using when evaluating your jetting by making some reference marks.

Install and USE an aftermarket fuel screw to get rid of the bogging, stumbling, and coughing at part-throttle operation.

CARB FAILURE

Considering that your carb is always working whenever the engine is running, it's surprisingly reliable. However, that doesn't mean zero-maintenance. The to-do list:

- Throttle cables get worn, dirty, dry (no lube), kinked, or damaged in a crash. Lube and adjust as detailed in your owner's manual. Sunline and Motion Pro make replacement cables that are better than stock.
- Slides move up and down and over time can become worn. Replace if you can see obvious signs of wear.
- Bike won't start? Check your four-stroke's carburetor hot start plunger. It will seize if not cleaned and lubed regularly—and it's a bear to get out if it has seized.
- If your bike is going to be sitting idle for more than a couple weeks, either drain all the fuel out of the carb via the drain in the float bowl, or start the bike up with the petcock off and run it dry. You do not want old gas sitting in your carb.
- At least once a racing season, pull the carb and go through it, cleaning out the jets and looking for problems.
- Stock up on some carb spare parts: needle clips, a few jets in both directions, and the screws that hold the float bowl.
- Did you bung up the Phillips screws trying to get the float bowl off? Use a needle-nose Vise-Grips to get it off. Then replace them with Allen head fasteners from your hardware store's metric selection.

MAKING SURE THE FUEL SCREW STAYS PUT

Aftermarket fuel screws sometimes work their way loose. You can make this less likely to happen by stretching the spring and adding a second O-ring so it sits tighter in the opening.

Fuel screws have a tendency to unscrew themselves. Add a second O-ring to make sure it doesn't.

PREMIX FACTS AND MYTHS

Two-stroke dirt bikes still have a lot going for them because maintenance and repair costs are significantly lower than for the four-stroke motors that are now the dirt bike majority. Premix is a two-stroke's go-juice, a combination of specially formulated oil and gasoline. Here's what you need to know to be a premix master:

- Use quality two-stroke oil specifically formulated for use in a dirt bike. In other words, do NOT use automotive engine oil, oil intended for outboard motors, chain saws, lawn trimmers, or anything other than motorcycles. This is the wrong place to try to save money.
- Proper ratio is important but your owner's manual recommendation may be too conservative. In general, a ratio of 24:1 to 32:1 is optimal and a good all-around baseline for bikes up to 125cc. For 250cc and above, you can run 32:1 to 50:1 ratios.
- Running more oil is not an advantage as it leads to combustion chamber coating and temperature increase, which then leads to detonation.
- Pour the oil into the gas can and then add fuel, not the other way around. Preferably do this the day you're riding, not before, so the oil doesn't have a chance to separate from the fuel, even though this isn't much of a problem these days.
- Mix just enough fuel for no more than a one- or two-week period. Fuel gets old fast. Don't fill the tank all the way up and think it's a way to save fuel for a long time. Your bike's tank is vented so the gas actually goes bad quicker than in a sealed gas can.
- See the gas ratio chart below; you can copy and tape it into your toolbox.
- Find a ratio and oil that works for your bike and stick with it. There's little point in brand-hopping as the name brand products are all good quality. Find one you like and that's readily available in your area and buy in quantity. From our experience, Yamalube R, Maxima M, and BelRay MC1 seem to be available just about everywhere.

Only use two-stroke oil designed for motorcycles, not for chain saws or outboard motors.

- It's a myth that two-stroke oil mixes better with race gas than the stuff you get from the pump. Don't believe it.
- Do NOT use aviation fuel. Despite the high octane number, it's totally unsuitable for use in a motorcycle for reasons too numerous to list here.
- Getting rid of old gas is a problem—one more reason to just buy what you need for each day of riding. Never just dump it onto the ground as it pollutes groundwater supplies and shows how ignorant you are. It's also against the law. Some cities have recycling drop-off sites for hazardous waste such as this, so call your local city officials. Another alternative is to fill a large metal tray with old newspaper and pour in the old gas. The newspaper absorbs the fuel and when dry, the newspaper can then be disposed in the regular trash.

TWO-STROKE PREMIX CHART

USA Measurement			Metric Measurement		
Gas/Oil Ratio	OZ per Gal	OZ per 4-Gal	CC per Gal	CC per 4-Gal	CC per Liter
20:1	6.4 oz	25.6 oz	189cc	756cc	50cc
24:1	5.3 oz	21.2 oz	158cc	632cc	41.7cc
32:1	4 oz	16 oz	118cc	472cc	31.3cc
40:1	3.2 oz	12.8 oz	95cc	380cc	25cc
50:1	2.6 oz	10.4 oz	76cc	304cc	20cc

Note: This chart is based on the fact that most oils are packaged in a size appropriate for a 4-gallon (USA) mix, even though most gas cans are 5-gallon capacity. If you need either more or less fuel, use the oz/gal or cc/liter numbers to adjust accordingly.

Here's how to clean an air filter. See the next page for more information. Label your three tubs so you know what's in them. Tub #1 gets the thankless job of peeling off the heaviest layers of dirt from the filter. You will be replenishing this tub regularly with clean kerosene or cleaner. Tub #2 is for final cleaning before washing, and #3 is for oiling the filter.

Dunk the clean filter in Tub #3 where you have your favorite filter oil. Squeeze out the excess back into the tub.

Whatever filter oil you choose—solvent based or water wash-up—follow the cleaning instructions. Never use gasoline to clean a filter, period.

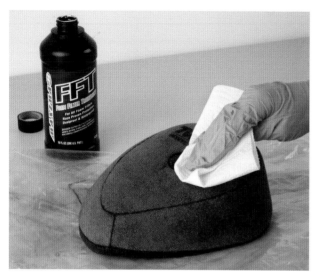

Pat the surface of the filter to soak up any excess and let the filter sit overnight before riding.

PUT IT ON THE CARB

Use a Sharpie to write your carb's jetting on the float bowl for easy reference. It also keeps you from tearing the carb apart to rejet, only to discover you're already running that particular jetting combination.

If you don't keep a log of your bike's settings—and you should—at least take the time to use a Sharpie to write the jetting information on the float for quick reference.

THE RIGHT WAY TO CLEAN AN AIR FILTER

Filters are your engine's first line of defense against dirt. Cleaning them is a ritual you shouldn't skip. And like everything else in life, there's a right way and a wrong way to do it. Filter oil comes in (eco) water-cleanup versions and in versions where solvent is needed for cleaning. With either, proper cleaning is similar. The correct method is a four-step process:

- Buy three small plastic tubs with lids—a one-gallon size is perfect. You can find something in the kitchen department of any big store, or the paint department of a hardware store. The tubs should be slightly larger and deeper than the filter.
- Label the lid of each tub so you know which is which.
- Fill tubs one and two half-full with kerosene or your preferred dedicated filter cleaner. Mineral spirits from the hardware store also works. Never use gas.
- Dump a full quart or so of filter oil into tub three and seal it tight.
- Wear nitrile gloves to protect your skin.
- You may want to remove the rubber gasket in the center of the filter, as the cleaners can harden this, which means it'll shrink and provide an opening for dirt to get in. It just pops in and out; there's no glue.
- Put the dirty filter in tub one and let it soak for a few minutes. Then dunk and gently squeeze out the filter until the worst of the dirt has come off. (Note that you can reuse the kerosene if you make a grid shelf from hardware cloth to fit in the bottom of the tub. Once the dirt settles, pour the still-good cleaner into a container and dump the sludge.)
- Move the filter to tub two and dunk and squeeze and work out any dirt still stuck to the foam. Gently squeeze it dry—do not wring it or tie it into knots.
- Although by now the filter looks pretty clean, it's not. You now need running water and some dishwashing soap. Squeeze some soap onto the filter and wash it in warm or hot running water. You will be amazed at how much dirt will still be in the filter—which is why cleaning the filter is a two-step process.
- Rinse and repeat until no more dirt particles or soap suds are visible. Rinse completely until there's no trace of soap left.
- Shake out the water and then put the filter aside to dry at least overnight or longer. I like to hook them onto the handlebar so they can drip dry.
- The only difference in this routine for eco-filters that can be washed in water is substituting water for the kerosene. Never throw one of these filters into a washing machine or dishwasher, even if your buddy tells you he does it ". . . all the time."

THE RIGHT WAY TO OIL AN AIR FILTER

Once a filter is clean and dry—really dry, as any damp spots will keep the filter oil from settling into the foam—you're ready to oil it. There are various ways to do this, but this is the method I prefer:

- Open tub three and dunk the filter into the filter oil. Let it soak it up. You may want to turn the filter inside-out first to ensure complete penetration on both sides of the filter, but it's not absolutely necessary.
- Squeeze out the excess back into the tub so that only a very light coat of oil remains, with the whole filter evenly coated. Again, you're squeezing it, not wringing the life out it.
- Put the filter back on its cage—which you have already cleaned—and set it on your workbench on top of some paper towels. Pat the surface of the filter with more paper towels to soak up any excess blobs of oil.
- Filter oil takes a while to set up and get tacky, so allow it to dry at least overnight before going riding.
- Apply some waterproof grease on the rim to further seal the filter against the airbox. Technically, modern filters shouldn't require the bead of grease as the foam rim is much wider than in the old days, but it's cheap insurance, costs nothing, and gives you one more barrier to keep out dirt.
- You can prepare multiple filters at the same time, storing the extras in plastic bags. However, only store oiled filters you intend to use within two weeks. Longer than that and some filter oils will start to dry out or pool.
- Filter oils that can be washed in soap and water should be used within about two weeks of oiling the filter, as these products don't seem to stay on the filter as long as the solvent-based filter oils. That's personal experience talking again.
- An alternate method to using the three tubs is to put the filter in a large plastic bag and pour in the filter oil and knead it into the filter. This method works fine, but any excess filter oil ends up wasted.
- Aerosol filter oil seems convenient, but coverage tends to be uneven and doesn't treat as many filters as using a liquid.
- Don't use motor oil as it will pass through the filter and into the motor. If you can't afford proper filter oil, you probably shouldn't be riding at all because you'll just end up with a worn-out engine.

FILTER DO'S AND DON'TS

Filters wear out. Figure 30 to 50 washings and they're ready for the trash. The best approach is to have two or three filters and rotate usage. At the first sign of worn foam, tears, or loose seams, throw the filter away.

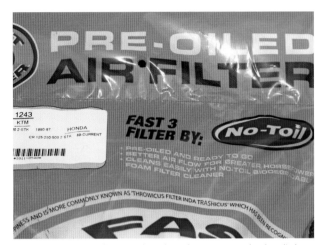

Packaged disposable air filters are nice to have along on race weekends as it gives you an easy way to pop on a fresh filter with little fuss. When removing from the package, knead the filter to redistribute any oil that has pooled and you may want to add a bit more if the filter seems too dry.

- **AGAIN! Never wash your filter in gasoline.** Today's pump gas is a highly toxic mixture of chemicals, many of which are known carcinogens. Gasoline also eats away the adhesives used to hold the filter together.
- Clean the inside of the airbox so there's no dirt waiting to fall into the carb intake. No Toil Airbox Cleaner works very well at this messy chore.
- The brass filter screen on four-stroke engines is there to prevent a backfire from starting a fire. If you remove the screen, use a special backfire-resistant air filter such as a Twin Air Power Flow or No Toil. Yes, the backfire threat is real and seeing your pride and enjoy going up in flames is not a pleasant experience.
- **REMEMBER**: Filters can be stored in a sealed plastic bag for a couple of weeks but longer than that and the oil tends to separate.
- Pre-oiled "disposable" filters (they can be cleaned and reused if you want) are a recent concept. It's good to have one of these in your spares box as a backup when heading out for a race weekend. With some brands, the oil tends to settle in one spot or the filter may not be quite as wet as you prefer, so it's smart to have some filter oil along to work into any bare spots.
- Filter skins provide an additional layer of filtering and are available for both very dusty and very wet conditions. They can be quickly removed, exposing the cleaner inner filter element. Twin Air makes a special cover specifically for muddy and wet conditions to reduce the risk of water getting into the carb.
- If a puddle appears under your airbox overnight, your filter is either over-oiled or you're using a filter oil that won't stick to your filter. In either case, take out the filter and squeeze out the excess or change your brand of filter oil.

Understand what the labels mean. The two you don't want to use are E-85 and methanol if you can avoid it.

FUELISH DECISIONS: AT THE PUMP

What to put into your bike's gas tank is both a personal and philosophical decision. I know riders that religiously only use expensive race gas; and just as many others pull up to the pump at the local Mega-Oil station and fill their gas cans with whatever comes out the nozzle. Here's the skinny:

- Always run at least 91 or higher octane gas.
- Higher octane numbers don't provide more power. Higher octane simply counters detonation and pinging.
- Fuel with up to 10 percent ethanol or alcohol is okay.
- Fuel with up to 15 percent MTBE is okay.

CHASING A LEAN POP

If you're getting popping/backfiring on deceleration, you've got a "lean pop." Get rid of it by checking for air leaks at the exhaust pipe header, especially if it's an aftermarket pipe. If it's cooler than normal or early morning, start with the fuel screw and richen things up. If you have an off-road bike with an air-injection system (CRF-X and WR-F models, for example), check there first. Plugging the AIS opening with some duct tape will tell you if it's the cause.

- You can use up to 15 percent methanol safely if there's no other choice, but it's better to avoid it because it makes the bike harder to start and eats rubber O-rings.
- E-85 should be avoided. It produces less power and will require rejetting.
- Two-strokes benefit more from higher octane than thumpers.
- Gas goes bad quickly. Only buy what you're going to use riding that day. If the bike and fuel can are going to sit for a couple weeks, pour in some Maxima Fuel Stabilizer in both the bike and the fuel can.
- Longer storage of fuel requires metal cans, not plastic. Plastic is porous, believe it or not, and fuel will evaporate enough to change its density.

THE TRUTH ABOUT RACE GAS

Race gas works, but that still doesn't mean you need to—or should—use it. The high-test facts of life:

- Race gas works; that's indisputable. However, the simple reality is that most of us, whether we're play riders or hard core amateur racers, simply don't need race gas. It's a luxury that few can justify.

All taxes included

MINIMUM OCTANE RATING
(R+M) / 2 METHOD
87

MINIMUM OCTANE RATING
(R+M) / 2 METHOD
89

(R+M) / 2 METHOD
93
PRESS

- If you're an up-and-coming pro rider who needs to dominate the local A class, then you're probably already using race gas. But at that level, you're likely receiving some sponsorship and if you're any good, you're collecting some cash instead of plastic trophies.
- Race gas will cost you from $6 to $15 per gallon depending on brand and formulation. If you're on any kind of a budget, a five-gallon can of race gas can set you back about the cost of a new rear tire, but that tire will last a lot longer and deliver more benefit.
- Use race gas if your bike detonates even when using the best available pump premium in your area, or if your bike is modified with a high-compression piston and other tweaks.
- Some types of race gas cannot be left in the bike for more than a week before they start to leave deposits or damage rubber parts. Draining it out after riding is one more chore to deal with.
- Mixing race gas $^{50}/_{50}$ with the pump stuff is common, but offers little benefit because you're diluting the race gas more than you're improving the pump stuff. Mixing the two makes sense when the local fuel is of low or questionable quality.

SERVICE THE HOT START PLUNGER . . . OR ELSE

The hot start plungers tucked away in the body of the Keihin FCR carb were originally brass and were easily damaged if any dirt or water got inside—and it did, running down the cable whenever you washed the bike. This led eventually to a stuck hot start plunger and a bike that wouldn't run. Newer versions of the Keihin FCR come with nickel-plated plungers that are less prone to seizing, but it still doesn't end the problems.

Like your girlfriend or wife, you gotta give it some loving, or it will go bad on you. Periodically remove the plunger from the carb, clean it, and then spray on some WD-40 or similar lube. Replace the easily broken stock plastic hot start fitting with an aluminum billet number from Zip-Ty Racing or Pro Circuit.

UNSTICKING A STUCK HOT START

There are some things in life you want to avoid: a corroded-in-place swingarm bolt is one, and a stuck hot start plunger is another. You can't use brute force to free a stuck hot start, because the part is small and a Keihin FCR carb is about $700 to replace if you mess things up. Here's how you do it:

Pump gas is like yogurt or a gallon of milk: It has a limited shelf life. Two weeks max. Add fuel stabilizer to the tank and the fuel jugs if they're going to be sitting for a few weeks between rides.

- If the lever doesn't move, squirt some cable lube or penetrating oil down the cable until you're sure it's reached the plunger. Use a cable luber so you don't make a mess of things.
- If it stays stuck, take the carb off and apply penetrating oil liberally to the plunger. Let it set for a while (overnight if possible) and cross your fingers.
- If it's still no go, take off the top of the carb and crank up your air compressor. Use compressed air to blow into the hole that the hot start uses and hope that it blows the plunger free.
- Another trick is inserting a small screwdriver into the plunger and gently twisting back and forth but not in complete circles. Be gentle, be careful.
- The main thing is to not damage the plunger cavity or you'll end up with a lovely $700 doorstop.

Chapter 9
Performance Modifications

If you're a good enough rider, you can win on a completely stock bike because today's bikes are virtually race-ready the moment you first pour some gas in the tank. That said, almost no one races a stock bike and your bank account is the only limiting factor in how much money you can spend. No matter how good it is straight from the factory, the urge to tweak, tune, decorate, and modify is a strong one. We're gearheads; it's what we do.

HOP IT UP: MODIFICATIONS AND MONEY

There are endless ways to modify a dirt bike. It's one of the joys of the sport, sort of like having a really great-looking girlfriend.

Some mods are best installed by people who know what they're doing (i.e., actual mechanics) because the consequences of making a mistake can be expensive. While most dirt bike products are designed to be installed by the rider, major motor or suspension work is best handled by writing a check to someone who has the tools and experience to do it correctly, sort out any problems that come up, and fine-tune the results.

Modifications fall into four broad categories: engine performance, suspension, looks, and ergos. Here are the pros and cons of various performance modifications, what you can expect to pay, and what you will get in return. But first, let's look at the two bargain approaches.

Andrew Short getting some practice laps in. *Simon Cudby/Throttle Jockey*

Ride a lot and you'll be faster. And it doesn't cost you anything.

ZERO-COST SPEED: $0

There are no bad bikes, just bad riders. If you want more speed, the no-cost secret is practice, practice, practice. Ride a lot, work on your techniques, practice your starts, learn how to use both brakes to their maximum, and discover how your bike responds to various conditions and setups. Ride on nice sunny days and gawd-awful muddy ones. Getting a lot of saddle time will make you faster than any bolt-on part possibly could. When you do pull out your wallet, spend your money on good tires and keeping the engine fresh.

NEW RUBBER: $60 TO $90 PER TIRE

The best speed secret of them all: *Run fresh tires*. Instead of spending your hard-earned moto-budget on titanium pipes, trendy graphics, and other eye candy, buy fresh rubber at every opportunity. Pro riders know this. Fresh tires let you come off the line harder, hit turns deeper, brake at the maximum, knife through mud and sand, and do all of the other things we expect a race bike to do. Learn how to change tires yourself and buy them in quantity to score a discount from your dealer. You can easily resell your barely used tires at the races to other riders who don't know this three-word secret and would rather save a few bucks than be faster.

Fresh meat on your wheels for every race is the *real* speed secret.

The Boyesen Power X-Wing smoothes out the turbulent airflow coming from the air box and increases its velocity as it enters the carb. The result is a crisper throttle response with no dips or sags.

If overheating is a problem, go up a notch on the radiator pressure cap. The number you see is between 1.1 and 1.4 kg/cm2 (kilograms per square centimeter is the metric equivalent to psi).

BETTER BREATHING: $150 TO $300

The better an engine can inhale, the more power it can make. For two-stroke riders, a Boyesen or V-Force reed cage provides a boost over the stock setup and is an easy change. At the minimum replace the stock reeds with Boyesen or Moto Tassinari versions. Reeds wear out so check them periodically and replace regularly before they affect performance.

For thumpers, Twin Air and No Toil both make air filter and case packages that eliminate the backfire screen on the stock cage—which may provide a little boost—and a better filter that's backfire resistant. You need spare filters anyhow, so buy ones that are backfire resistant.

The Keihin FCR carbs can be improved by adding a Boyesen Power X-Wing to the inlet tract portion of the carb (it just slips in). The X-Wing takes the tumbling mass of air coming through the air filter and straightens it out as it enters the carb. This increases air velocity and therefore, power. Throttle response and a smoother transition from the low-end to midrange is an added benefit. You'll feel it as a crisper response with no dips or sags in the powerband. The Boyesen Power X-Wing fits inside the rubber air boot and requires no modification to install. Yes, it's simple, and yes, it works. One will set you back about $125—money well spent.

ENGINE MODS AND BIG-BORE KITS: $300 ON UP (WAY UP)

An entire book could (and maybe should) be written that deals only with engine modifications. There are so many possible changes that trying to pin down what modifications justify their cost is impossible. Some guidelines:

- It's not that difficult to get more than 60 horsepower out of a modern 450F, but unless you're an elite rider of boundless skill, a hillclimber, ride nothing but sand dunes, or weigh more than 250 pounds, you probably don't need that much power. The limiting factor is traction. Too much power simply gets thrown away as wheelspin when you're riding in the dirt.
- The best time for any engine performance work is when you're going into the motor for some essential maintenance. It's a good time to see if you can justify spending more on additional performance via more radical cams, head porting, stiffer valve springs, or a bigger piston.
- If you ride a 250cc four-stroke in a Vet or an age class where there's no displacement restriction, a big-bore kit is your new best friend. These kits will push the engine up to around 280cc and are easily worth the $500 to $750 they cost. The additional engine capacity provides a substantial power boost and reliability isn't usually affected. For about half this amount, you can bump up a 250 two-stroke to about the same size with the same pleasing results. Athena, Wiseco, and many other firms offer big-bore kits.

Boost your bike's cooling efficiency by using special coolants.

- Head porting/polishing, different cams/valves, higher compression, and special forged pistons are all expensive in themselves and having someone who knows what he's doing install those parts and tune the resulting package to your satisfaction adds to the total. Expect to pay a minimum of $1,000 for motor modifications from a shop.

COOL IT OFF: $15 TO $500

Heat is the enemy of reliability and today's four-strokes are hot enough to fry your breakfast eggs. You actually want your bike to run hot, because a four-stroke is producing the most power when it reaches a certain operating temperature. The trick is to keep it from getting too hot, because that's when things start to go wrong. Some ways to keep the heat under control:

- Run Engine Ice, Maxima Cool-aide, Liquid Performance, WaterWetter, or similar products that boost the efficiency of the cooling system.

- Never run straight coolant without water. It should be a $^{50}/_{50}$ mix of coolant and distilled or deionized water. Don't use tap water—it has too many minerals in it and that's bad for the radiator. A gallon of distilled water from the grocery store is $2. Add WaterWetter to improve its cooling ability. WaterWetter is a mix of rust inhibitors, surface-tension reducing surfactants, and waterpump lubricants that literally makes water better. You only need four ounces to treat a gallon of water.

- A Boyesen Hy-Flo Water Pump Impeller kit costs about $200 but increases coolant flow by about 20 percent thanks to the more efficient impeller design. Because it is more efficient it puts less drag on the engine, which is like getting free horsepower in the bargain. This is an especially useful mod on 250F motors, which are more stressed and more prone to overheating than 450F engines.

- Coolant is not the same as antifreeze, although anything with glycol in it provides some antifreeze capability. If you live where it's extremely cold in the winter and the bike is in an unheated area, don't assume the coolant will provide protection. You may need to flush the cooling system out each year when you put the bike to bed for the season.

- Do not use automotive coolant in your bike as its formula is more abrasive than motorcycle coolants and can lead to waterpump seal failure.
- Coolant wears out. Drain and renew your radiator's contents at least once a season.
- If overheating is a regular event, go to a higher pressure radiator cap from your dealer. However, don't go up more than one notch in radiator cap pressure as higher pressures are tough on seals, hoses, and radiators.
- Switch to silicone radiator hoses. They're more durable than OEM pieces, come in colors, and the smoother inner hose allows coolant to move faster. Kits with pre-cut pieces to fit the most common bikes are about $75 to $190 depending on model.
- Larger and sturdier radiators are expensive (about $300 to $450) but a good choice if you damage a stock radiator.

Silicone radiator hoses are stronger than OEM, move coolant more efficiently, and look cool.

The aftermarket units are larger, hold more coolant, are more efficient, and are simple bolt-ons with no modifications.

- If you're a pro or want the ultimate in cooling systems, there are now aftermarket radiators with built-in oil coolers. These elaborate systems significantly drop engine operating temperatures but at a cost of nearly $1,000.
- Get more air moving through the radiator with Lightspeed's carbon fiber winglets. The old "ram air" idea put to work on a motocross bike.
- Keep your fuel cool by means of carbon fiber heat shields or flexible heat barrier fabrics. Mostly these are defenses against heat from the exhaust pipe as it travels past the carb and cooks the gas.

LESS MASS = MORE SPEED

Light is good and even lighter is better. The factories are well aware that a lighter bike will also be a faster bike, everything else being equal. Today's machines are miracles of lightweight construction, but if cost wasn't a factor, they could be even lighter.

Well, what the factory can't do, you can. Here's how to slim down your ride:

- If you're serious about this, you need to weigh things accurately, so buy a digital postal scale that reads up to at least 5 pounds, but 20 pounds would be better. You can buy them on eBay for $20.
- Focus on unsprung weight (the suspension, wheels, and other components directly supported by the suspension) because losing 1 pound here is the same as dropping 6 pounds of sprung weight.
- Focus on big items, not the little stuff. For example, a lighter axle saves proportionally more weight with less effort than replacing a bunch of fasteners.
- For motocross, you don't need heavy-duty tubes. Run lighter/thinner tubes or switch to the Nu-Tech Tubeless tire system which can save from 1 to 3 pounds per wheel.
- Some tires are significantly heavier than others. Drag them onto the scale and see for yourself. The difference between brands can be significant—as much as a pound for a rear tire.
- Also put your rims, chain, sprockets, spokes, fasteners, axles, and linkage pieces on the scale. For most of these components, there's nothing you can reasonably do to make them lighter, but the rims, chain, and sprockets are obvious places to look for lighter alternatives.
- Starting at the top for sprung weight (technically "sprung mass"), do you have every inch of the bike covered in decals? Those can add 2 pounds.
- Some brands of plastic are lighter than others. Put them on the scale and if the weight saving is worth it, switch out all the body plastic.

Make your bike feel lighter by lowering the radiators. DRD makes radiator-lowering kits for a variety of race bikes. No modifications needed; just unbolt, install the kit, reinstall the radiators.

An O-ring chain is the no-fuss choice, but it brings with it a weight penalty. This one is a half-pound heavier than a comparable standard (no O-ring) motocross chain.

- Carbon fiber and titanium fasteners have a considerable coolness factor but contribute little to overall weight loss except in terms of making your wallet lighter. However, there's no penalty attached either, so indulge yourself if the cost doesn't stop you.
- Lose the beer gut. If you're 20 pounds or more overweight, start going to a gym, work with a trainer, and most important, improve your diet. Stop going through the drive-through window. Get healthy, get strong, and get lean.

PIPES: $300 TO $1000

Exhaust pipes are the sexy add-on, and back when we all rode two-strokes, everyone bought aftermarket pipes because they provided a cheap ($200) performance boost. Four-strokes have changed the equation, however, and today a top-of-the-line exhaust system can set you back as much as $800. The facts:

- You're rarely going to get a huge weight saving over stock, even with the titanium and carbon fiber systems. In most cases, you will be saving ounces, not pounds, with most of the metal dieting coming from the muffler. My stock CRF450 exhaust weighed only 2 ounces more than the high-zoot aftermarket system I installed.
- Titanium head pipes ding easily from roost. If you're buying a ti system, be sure the manufacturer offers the head pipe separately in case you need a replacement. Not all of them do.
- A titanium pipe offers no performance boost that you can't get from the identical pipe in stainless steel.

- Carbon fiber mufflers are expensive and not especially durable. They tend to develop cracks after a while.
- Stainless-steel pipes with an aluminum muffler are the best choice in terms of price, performance, durability, and weight.
- Performance gains or changes are hard to identify or quantify. When the magazines do dyno tests for pipe comparison stories, it's not uncommon for the stock OEM pipe to be a good all-around compromise of weight, sound, and power. This only makes sense as the

HOW TO TELL IF THE MOTOR IS TIRED

Catch the little problems early to prevent them from becoming bigger and more expensive problems. Warning signs that the engine needs some attention:

- On CRFs, more than an inch of oil collects in the breather tube (the clear tube with a plug in it running under the carb) between motos. Other brands have their breather tubes exiting in other locations.
- The bike gets easier and easier to kick over as if—gasp!—there's no compression.
- The oil level keeps dropping faster than usual.
- You think the motor feels tired and not as powerful as in the past.
- You haven't done more than the bare minimum of maintenance, if that.
- It won't kick start easily or at all, but starts and runs fine when pushed or pull-started. This is a sign of low compression.

An aftermarket pipe can be an expensive tweak. Be sure you're getting one that delivers what you need in terms of power delivery.

factories focus on getting the most from their motor. Still, the right pipe can provide a noticeable improvement over stock. The trick is figuring out which pipe you need.

- Aftermarket pipes make more power by borrowing it from other portions of the powerband. You lose a little top-end rev but gain in the mid-range or vice-versa. Be leery of massive horsepower claims.
- DO NOT buy a new pipe in order to get something louder. Noise is killing dirt biking and closing down tracks. The race organizations are responding (finally) with stricter noise requirements and sound tests on race day. Loud pipes are annoying, don't produce more power, and are going to kill motocross and off-road racing if we don't rein things in.
- A rule of thumb: Buy pipes from the aftermarket companies that are the choice of the top pros for your bike brand. These guys can run whatever they choose and they provide feedback to the companies for improvements. Pro Circuit, for example, still sells a lot of KTM 250 two-stroke pipes that were the result of Jeremy McGrath's brief KTM factory ride.
- A great pipe on an out-of-tune, poorly jetted, worn-out engine with a bad clutch is not going to magically improve the whole package.
- With electronic fuel injection (EFI) now becoming common, some riders have found that their EFI black box can't adjust and compensate for the aftermarket pipe.

DENTED TWO-STROKE PIPE

One of racing life's little tragedies is discovering a ding or outright humongous dent in your two-stroke's expansion chamber. This usually comes within hours of installing a new pipe. Just like new cars attract door dings, a new pipe attracts rocks and crashes. What you need to know:

- Minor dings and small dents may not affect anything more than top-end power.
- The worst dent is one in the first 6 inches of the exhaust pipe. If the pipe is essentially flattened or the dent very deep/large in that first half-foot, replace the pipe or have the dent pulled out and repaired.
- Dents in the center cone portion of the pipe have little effect on performance.

Disassemble the end cap and muffler body. This may require some force, but don't overdo things.

After removing the old packing and cleaning the core, slide the new packing onto the core and into the end cap. If there's excess material after stuffing it as full as possible, trim it off.

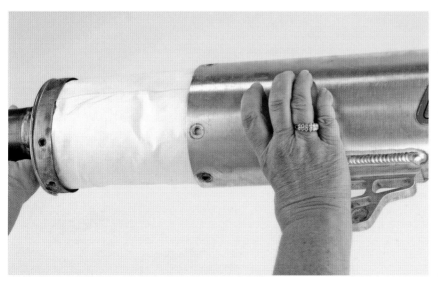

Reassemble the end cap and muffler body and reinstall fasteners or rivets. Use some RTV silicone seal to complete the job and make it more difficult for water to get in.

REPACK YOUR SILENCER

Want to gain back some lost horsepower? Then repack your silencer. A silencer with blown-out packing will have lost as much as three horsepower in the process. Thumpers need their muffler repacked more often than two-strokes because of the higher heat the four-banger puts out. Replace the packing every 30 hours or sooner. Noise never equals power when it comes to dirt bikes. Here's how to fix things:

- You will need a wire brush, muffler repacking kit (do not use steel wool or fiberglass insulation), soft mallet, ratchet or drill for the muffler's fasteners, and some high-temperature sealant from the auto parts store.
- Remove the screws or drill out the rivets to get the end cap off.
- Use the rubber mallet to gently tap the muffler body free. Chances are it'll be stubborn, but don't go all Kong on it and whale away.
- When the muffler body is off, remove the old packing and then clean the core with a wire brush. A clean core absorbs more noise.
- Slide the repacking kit over the core and make sure to slide it into the end cap. Most repacking kits come with a cardboard core to help you guide the packing over the core and into the end cap.
- Assemble the muffler body to the end cap. Apply thread-lock to fasteners and/or replace the rivets (any hardware store sells Pop-Rivets) and complete the assembly.
- Seal the end cap with RTV silicone sealant to complete the job.

WHERE TO SPEND YOUR PAYCHECK

An old cliche: "Speed costs money. How fast do you want to go?" Here's where the different options rank in terms of bang for buck, from best to worst.

True race gas (VP Fuels, for example) is the quickest way to a noticeable horsepower increase—just pour and go. However, along with the per-gallon expense, you can't leave these fuels in your carb for long, which means draining it out at the end of race day.

For the play rider or bucks-down weekend warrior who still wants to be competitive on the track, a two-stroke offers a lower cost to race and is cheaper to modify. A four-stroke is exactly the opposite situation, with a higher cost to buy, maintain, and modify because there are simply more moving parts to deal with. Thumpers also require a higher level of mechanical skill to make engine modifications.

More bark, more bite . . . for a price.

Two-Strokes

1	Big-bore kit (if legal for the classes you ride)	$300 plus installation
2	Expansion chamber	$200-plus
3	Race gas—liquid horsepower	$12 per gallon
4	Port, polish, match cases, etc.	$200 minimum

Four-Strokes

1	Race gas—liquid horsepower	$12 per gallon
2	Aftermarket pipe	$500-plus
3	Big-bore kit (if legal for your class)	$500 to $800 plus installation
4	Higher compression piston	$150 plus installation
5	High performance cams	$200 to $400 plus installation

Chapter 10
Dirt Bike Savvy: Buying and Taking Care of Your Stuff

Having dirt bikes is like having kids. They require a lot of time and personal attention and they can be damn expensive, usually at the worst possible time for your budget. Here's how to take care of your stuff so it lasts as long as possible.

TIE IT DOWN PROPERLY

Transporting your bike(s) should be as simple yet as secure as possible. No matter what vehicle you're using, holding the bike comes down to two choices: tie-downs or bike shoes.

Davi Millsaps. *Simon Cudby/Throttle Jockey*

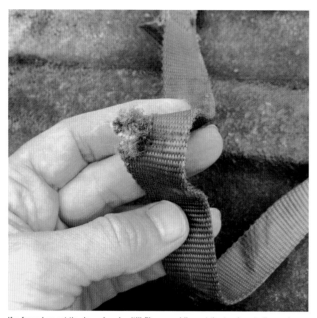

If a frayed or cut tie-down breaks, it'll fling your bike out the truck or trailer and create an expensive mess in the road.

Four tie-downs, two to a side, mean the forks don't have to be compressed as much and you don't have to worry about one breaking or coming loose. Yeah, it's overkill, but it's also cheap insurance.

- Get good ones. Ancra is what I trust. Cheapie tie-downs make me nervous.
- Tie-downs wear out, fray, get cut, and can (and will, at the worst possible time) break, leaving $7,000 worth of motorcycle lying in colorful pieces all over the road. Periodically, check your tie-downs for fraying, cuts, or loose threads, and replace them if necessary. (Or give them to that other racer who's always beating you.)
- Use two tie-downs per side on the forks. It's cheap insurance against a broken tie-down and having them doubled-up means the forks don't have to be compressed as much.
- Fork supports or braces that supposedly keep the fork springs from sacking out when tied down are useless because modern fork springs don't really sack out. If you want to use something, use a small inflatable ball (a soccer or volleyball) between the wheel and the fender when you compress the forks.
- Only hauling one bike? The correct way is to put the bike in your pickup on the driver's side so you have an unobstructed view to the rear. That said, almost nobody does it this way, preferring to put the bike in the middle of the truck bed.
- A wheel chock or one of the bars that hold the front wheel in a notch should be on your "buy" list because they keep the front wheel from shifting.
- Have a trailer and hate hassling with tie-downs? Then get a bike shoe. These work by clamping the front wheel and tire in place without compressing the forks. The gotcha is that they don't work on all bike sizes, don't work with street bikes because of their fenders, take up a lot of room, and at about $95 each, aren't exactly a bargain. They can also be installed in your truck bed.

HOW TO WASH YOUR RIDING GEAR

You probably have about $1,000 or so wrapped up in riding gear and maybe twice that much. Boots, a good helmet, pants, goggles, a Leatt neck brace, pads, and all the rest of the stuff you need—plus a bag to hold it all—quickly adds up. Taking care of your gear means you can get your money's worth out of it. Let's jump into this feet first.

Boots

- The key to boot care is to clean them as soon as possible to keep mud from drying or staining the leather. Knock mud off the sole and sides and then hose them down. Use a nylon brush—not a wire one—to dislodge any clumps.
- Just use a hose—not a power washer—to get the mud off. The pressure washer drives the water into the leather and prematurely wears them out.
- A traffic cone is a good way to hold a boot for washing or drying. You can buy them at the home improvement stores.
- Let wet boots dry out before you put them away. Feet sweat so riding leaves the boots soggy. Set them out in

the sun—but not for days on end—or stuff newspaper or paper towels inside to suck up moisture.

- Periodically apply some leather-care product to keep the leather portions of the boot from getting stiff.
- After washing and drying out, spray WD-40 on the buckles.
- Boots are best stored flat on their sides in your gear bag so that gravity can't go to work on them and make them saggy.
- Before riding in deep mud, spray your boots with some Pam or WD-40 to keep mud from sticking.
- Buy a boot that offers replacement parts. Not all of them do. Some also have repair services and there are a number of companies that can replace the sole as it gets torn up from the footpegs.

Pants

- If they're especially mucky, hose them off first before putting them in the washing machine.
- Learn how to do your own riding gear laundry. Your mom/wife/girlfriend will appreciate it, scoring you valuable brownie points, and you'll always have clean gear when you need it.
- Use an Oxy-Clean type detergent and set the washer on heavy dirt.
- Spray stain remover on especially nasty spots before washing.
- The sooner you can get your gear into the washer, the better, but you'll probably encounter some mud that will stain despite multiple washings. White gear stains easier than colors.
- Jerseys can go into the dryer if you're short of time, but pants should always be hung up to drip dry. Jerseys should be hung to dry if there's time.
- Because most pants now have a large leather or chamois area on the leg for burn protection, don't let them soak in water too long.

Helmets

- Remove the inner liner and cheek pads and rinse in clean water to remove the sweat buildup. A bit of shampoo will make it smell better.
- A fabric softener sheet wiped around the inside of your helmet kills the sweaty smell.
- Don't use any cleaning products on the helmet liner (the padding) that might irritate you when you're sweating.
- As with boots, it's better to get mud off as soon as you can. To keep mud from sticking, spray on some Maxima SC1 or similar detailing product.
- Never dry a helmet in front of a fire or oven. Let it sit in the sun, inside portion facing up.
- A great product is the Shock Doctor (www.shockdoctor.com) helmet dryer. Not only does it safely and conveniently dry a sweaty helmet (and other gear), you can buy a version

A traffic cone makes a convenient stand for washing/drying boots. Buy them at the big box home improvement stores.

A laundry softener sheet wiped around the helmet liner kills the sweaty smell.

The Shock Doctor helmet dryer is a convenient way to dry out helmets and other pieces of riding gear.

For wet and muddy days, this is what you need: an old goggle lens taped to the front of the visor to extend it, Roll-Offs and gloves with gripper strips of rubber on them (any hardware store).

that pumps ozone into the helmet to neutralize odors and bacteria.

- Never use contact spray or brake cleaner on a helmet shell.
- Any kind of good wax can be used to keep the helmet shiny and help keep mud from sticking.
- Smelly helmet? Spray some Febreze inside. In fact, carry some in your gear bag.
- When cleaning your helmet, look for signs of crash damage and wear. You should replace your helmet every few years in any case. A crash that knocks you out means it's time for a new helmet. Most of the name-brand helmet makers offer an evaluation service to determine if a helmet has sustained too hard a hit.

Goggles

- Despite an oft-repeated myth, goggles should never be tossed into a washing machine. The washing action eats up the foam. Wash them by hand in the sink and then hang up to drip dry.
- Sweat eats goggle foam, so wash the goggles regularly to prolong their useful life.
- Even with careful washing, the foam wears out and you'll need to replace the goggles after a while.

Gloves

- Since today's gloves are mostly synthetic fibers with little or no leather, they can simply be thrown in the washing machine and then hung up to drip dry.

SEE WHERE YOU'RE GOING

We've all got them and we all need them. Here's how to make your goggles earn their keep:

- Use an anti-static spray to keep dust and grime from sticking, which also makes the dust easier to remove with a quick finger swipe. Use Endust or Static Guard (swipe it from your wife/GF) and spray both sides of the lens.
- When using tear-offs, put the bottom one on the right-hand side so you'll still have one tear-off left if you accidentally pull off all the others with one yank.
- Didn't bring along any anti-fog treatment? Use a piece of soap. Rub it into the inside of the lens, let it dry, and then polish it out until all the haze is gone.
- If fogging is a constant problem, invest in some dual-pane goggles that skiers and snowmobilers use.
- In wet conditions, if you have Roll-Offs, you must use a visor on the lens or the film will stick to the lens and tear. No visor? Use a strip of duct tape, folding over one edge so it's thicker and attach it to the top of the lens.
- If it's raining, treat goggles with Rain-X to keep the water from beading up.
- Stash a pair of inexpensive clear plastic safety glasses in your gear bag and when conditions are really ugly, use them instead of your expensive goggles. They won't fog up as easily and if they get totally covered in muck, you can toss them away without feeling like you're setting fire to your wallet.
- Apply a thin bead of Vaseline on the inside of the bottom goggle frame to catch and hold any dirt, sand, and other debris that gets trapped inside the goggles. This keeps the grit out of your eyes.
- Set up your Roll-Off equipped goggles to also accept a top layer of tear-offs for when things are really ugly out there. This is perfect for when the mud is flying hard at the start.

Might need to do a little cleaning up after this one.

- Apply a small amount of baby oil to the filter foam at the top of your goggles in order to trap dust before it gets inside. Use a swab to do this. Don't overdo the oiling or it'll be dripping down into the goggles while you ride.
- If the goggle strap keeps slipping on your helmet, put some beads of silicone seal on the inside of the strap at the back or use a hot glue gun. When dry, they'll grip the back of the helmet better.

TIME FOR A NEW HOME:
HOW TO GET YOUR BIKE READY FOR SALE

There comes a day when you're ready for a new ride. Naturally, you first have to sell the old bike and you want top dollar when you do. You'll want to start out by doing some research so you have a feel for what comparable bikes are selling for in your area—and only in your area. Check out the bikes in the classifieds, local dealer showrooms, at your favorite racetrack, craigslist.com, eBay, motorcycletrader.com, and any other sources that come to mind. Tell your buddies that you're selling and ask them to spread the word.

Now get the bike ready to dazzle prospective buyers. Here's what you need to do to make your old bike sell for the best price:

- Get it clean! Dedicate a day to detailing the bike. Don't just squirt it with a hose. You want the most thorough cleaning job you can manage, one that also involves fixing any problems, changing the oil, cleaning the air filter, and replacing worn plastic or graphics. By the end of the day your old bike may look so good you may not want to sell it.
- Clean underneath the bike. Flop down on your back and clean off baked-on ooze and crusted dirt. There's a lot of gunk trapped down there, so dig it out.
- Use Shout laundry cleaner and a hose to clean things off instead of a power washer. Be careful if you use a power washer (see Chapter 1) as you can do as much damage as good.
- When it's as clean as humanly possible, use some Maxima SC1 detail spray to polish up the plastic. Pledge wood polish works too. A clean bike sells for more money than a dirty one and sells quicker.
- Looks are important. If you've got mismatched or badly damaged plastic, replace it. You can buy complete replacement plastic kits for about $85 to $120 and it'll pay you back more than that in resale value. When I get a brand new bike, I often take off some of the stock plastic with fresh graphics—typically the radiator shrouds—and replace it with aftermarket pieces/graphics. When it comes time to sell, the stock pieces get reinstalled and it looks like a brand new bike again.
- Take off any expensive aftermarket parts that you want to use on the new bike or that you believe won't add much value to your used bike. Aftermarket pipes, fancy wheels,

Start your selling with an online listing. It's an easy way to get a lot of advertising for what you have to sell.

and such are good bets for resale on eBay or craigslist since at the most you're only going to get about half their original cost—if that—if left on the bike.
- When writing your ad or online listing, don't lie. Don't claim it's "lightly used" if you've been flogging it every weekend at the local track. Be honest and put yourself in the buyer's position. It's better to be truthful about the bike's condition than to let it spoil a sale or cause a dispute. More information is better than less. Anticipate what the questions will be and put the information in your listing/ad.
- Take digital photos and have them available to send via email. Not just full-bike shots from a distance, but also close-ups of various details. Take pictures of both sides of the bike.
- When you have a likely buyer coming to visit, have the bike displayed as favorably as possible. Put it dead center in your garage with a light overhead. Have all the accessories you're including nearby. Have the owner's manual on hand. If your garage is a cluttered junkyard, clean it up.
- Be willing to negotiate. Few things are more annoying than having a seller who won't budge a dime on price. That's just no fun. No need to give it away, but you should be willing to accept a reasonable offer. Remember that your goal is to get it sold.
- Only consent to a test ride if you feel confident the person knows how to ride and has riding gear along and a driver's license for you to hold onto.
- Don't be rushed into accepting an offer unless it all sounds and feels right to you. The old "I've got the cash in

my pocket" routine shouldn't by itself be a deal-maker.

- Have the bike's paperwork available. Title, if any, bill of sale from a dealer, and whatever documentation you have. If there's a lien on it, the lien will have to be taken care of before the title can be transferred.
- Know what price you want and what you'll accept—the second number should be lower. This is where you've got negotiating room and where your earlier research pays off.
- Be careful. If you get bad vibes from talking to the buyer—any negatives at all that make you wary—trust your gut instinct. Dirt bikes are a favorite target of thieves because they're seldom titled and are easy to resell. Have other people at the house when the would-be buyers visit—a neighbor or riding buddy. Have someone write down their license plate number if you're feeling especially cautious.
- Never meet a buyer by yourself in some secluded spot to do the deal. Only accept cash or a certified cashier's check from a local bank and in the proper amount. Copy down the buyer's driver's license number, address, phone number, and other details.

HOW TO START AND SURVIVE YOUR FIRST RACE

A lot of people ride dirt bikes, but only about one-third actually race in organized events. That's too bad, because racing is huge fun, besides giving you a way to compare your riding skills against others in a safe, objective way. There are as many reasons for not having raced as there are riders, but if you want to race, here's how to get started:

- Find some local tracks. Your dealer or riding buddies can point you toward them. Call, email, or visit them and ask about available classes, what paperwork they require if you're under age 18, what time the gates and sign-up open, what race organization membership is required, and so on.
- You don't need the latest and greatest bike. Race what you have and what you're used to. Your first few races are learning experiences, not an audition for a factory ride.
- You will need numbers. If you have to become a member of a race organization or AMA district, they'll probably assign you a number. If not, pick something with three digits and put it on your plates.
- If your bike has a sidestand or lights, remove them.
- Show up early on race day and get in line for sign-up early. If you're under 18, you'll probably need a parent with you at sign-up, plus a copy of your birth certificate, which may need to be notarized. (This is why you call the track ahead of time and ask questions.) Bring cash for your entry fees and if you're in line and not sure if you have the right entry forms, ask some of the other riders.
- Have the proper riding gear. Buy it used, borrow it from friends, or whatever you need to do to equip yourself

with adequate safety gear. You need a good helmet, good motocross boots, riding pants (not jeans), kidney belt, chest protector, goggles, and gloves as a minimum. Don't worry about being trendy or color-coordinated or if the gear is old, just so long as it's usable.

- Walk the track before practice. This is another reason you need to arrive early. You need to see what's out there at a walking pace, because the practice session will pass in a blur of too many riders and mass general confusion.
- Ride your proper practice session. This will be announced or posted and as a newbie, you should swallow your pride and ride with the slowest group out there. Don't ride the A or Pro practice session thinking you'll learn the hot lines—even if you could recognize those lines, you probably lack the skills to hit them at the right speed.
- Practice is not a race. Repeat: Practice is NOT a race. Ride practice to find out where the lines are, what speeds you need for corners and jumps, and to get comfortable with having traffic around you. But be very careful during practice as the differences in speed between riders can produce some nasty accidents.
- Go to the riders' meeting. Listen to what they tell you about the day's schedule, classes, changes, and so on. Bring a notebook so you can write down the race order since this typically isn't finalized until late.
- Watch the start of a race from the starting line. You need to get a feel for the pace of things, how and when to line up, what the procedures are, etc.
- Watch a race or two, but allow yourself about 30 minutes to prepare for your moto. (If you're riding an enduro or hare scrambles, all of this advice still applies, but the sequence of events will be different.)
- Preflight your bike. Clean off the number plates, make sure there's enough gas for the number of laps you're riding, and check for obvious problems. Check tire pressure as well (see Chapter 3).
- Race days start early and end late so come prepared with some shade, chairs, a cooler with drinks and sandwiches, plus whatever else you need to get through the day. If there's time, sit down and take it easy. Drink some water (not fizzy, sugared pop).
- Get to the start line for your race early. Get into your starting spot when directed, take some deep breaths, and try to relax. In between a few moments of sheer terror and confusion, you're going to have a lot of fun.
- Go out, race at your speed, attempting the jumps and other obstacles you're comfortable with. HOLD your line through corners (the faster riders will get around you without any help) rather than wandering from side to side.
- Most important, have fun. Have a friend or family member tape and photograph you. Those will be photos you'll treasure all your life.

DIRT BIKE STORAGE

If you have to store your bike for the off-season or much longer, follow these steps and you'll be able to quickly return it to race-ready service with no problems from the storage period.

1. Wash the bike thoroughly and then start it up and drive it around to warm up the engine and burn off trapped moisture so it's thoroughly dry. Spray some WD-40 on the chain, peg pivots, shifter, and all exposed metal surfaces to displace moisture and prevent corrosion. Never put a wet and dirty motorcycle away for a long nap or waking it back up will be very expensive.

2. Put new oil in the bike. Used oil contains moisture and contaminants that will cause damage if left sitting too long.

3. Inflate the tires to 15 or 20 psi and put the bike up on a stand so both tires are off the floor. If a tire still touches, put a piece of plywood under the tire.

4. Lube the chain. If you're worried about drips, put some newspaper underneath.

5. Fill the gas tank full and add fuel stabilizer. Now start the bike and let it run long enough so the stabilizer gets all the way through the fuel lines and carb. Top off the tank again—a full tank leaves less room for condensation to form.

6. Loosen the drain plug in the bottom of the carb and let the fuel drain out of the bowl.

7. Plug the muffler with either a rubber plug, some duct tape, or a shop rag. Rodents and birds have been known to set up housekeeping inside a muffler.

8. Top off the brake master cylinders to prevent moisture buildup. If the fluid is old, flush it out and replace with fresh fluid (see Chapter 3).

9. If it has a battery, put it on a battery tender (about $20) to keep it charged. A battery tender monitors the battery and keeps it charged; a regular trickle charger will eventually boil dry or overcharge a battery if left attached too long.

10. If the bike will be in storage for more than three months, remove the spark plug and pour a couple ounces of clean engine oil through the spark plug hole into the engine. Kick the engine over several times to spread the oil around and then reinstall the plug.

11. If the bike will be stored for more than three months, drain the radiators and water pump.

12. Cover the bike, even if it's with just an old blanket, to keep dust from collecting.

13. Generally, there's no point to starting up the bike periodically during the off-season unless you can ride it long enough so it's thoroughly warmed up.

When you're ready to ride again, drain out the oil and refill. Top off the radiators, install a fresh spark plug (never hurts), add fresh gas, and you're good to go.

Don't think that starting the bike every week or so and letting it run for a few minutes is an acceptable alternative because all that does is add more moisture and contaminants to your engine oil. You'd have to run the bike for an hour or more to burn off the moisture.

RACING ON A BUDGET

If your wife or girlfriend (or both of them) is giving you a hard time about what your racing is costing, here are some ways to cope:

1. Switch to a two-stroke. A top-end job that you can do yourself is $150 or less; a four-stroke top-end rebuild at your dealer will be $400 or more. Some tracks and race organizations now offer a "vintage" or non-current class for bikes that are at least five years old. If your favorite track doesn't, talk to them about adding it. In the right hands, a modern 250cc two-stroke is still competitive compared to a 450cc thumper. Also consider going big. A two-stroke, big-bore kit that gives you 280 or 300cc is often money well spent.

2. Help out. Tracks are always looking for help, whether it's waving a yellow flag, working sign-up, scoring, or replacing toilet paper in the porta-johns. In most cases there's either payment or freebies such as admission, concession stand lunch, or similar rewards. Make yourself useful in exchange for some work and you could be riding for free.

3. Rubber not bling. When you're on a budget, spend your money on fresh tires rather than a new pipe or other foof. Fresh tires will do more for your race results than any other one thing. Plus you can resell the hardly used old tires at the races.

Get together with your riding buddies and see if your dealer will give you a good discount on a quantity of tires or a case of oil if purchased all at once.

4. Get sponsored. You don't have to be the next Ricky Carmichael to get sponsored. If you're a regular customer at your dealer, ask whether they have any sponsorship programs. Surf over to www.sponsorhouse.com for help in finding potential sponsors. Ask your employer or your favorite local restaurant or bar whether they'd like to get their name in front of potential customers. The main thing about getting sponsored is to simply ask around, race résumé in hand. Be ready to explain how you'll represent your sponsor—just putting their decal on the bike isn't going to cut it.

5. Race for dollars. The manufacturers regularly offer cash contingency awards at many tracks. Of course you have to be riding a new bike to qualify. Find out which tracks host these races and become a regular. We know a number of riders who cover all their racing expenses this way.

6. Write it up. *Cycle News* is just one of several publications or online sites that will pay you a small amount in exchange for an understandable race report and a few photos. If you've got some basic writing skills and a camera, contact these publications and ask for their writer's guidelines. In addition, some tracks will pay you (or offer free race entries) in exchange for doing a story on their events.

7. Buy last year's model. Whether it's a bike or riding gear, get last year's model. This is especially true for riding gear, since few of us can tell (or care) whether you're wearing this year's trendy look or last year's fashion disaster.

8. Do it yourself. Working on a four-stroke motor is more complex than a two-stroke, but it's not nuclear physics. Start with a shop manual and acquire the skills as your bike requires work.

9. Max out your tires. Give up some traction by buying rear tires that have a reputation for being long-wearing (Maxxis is one). When the knobs get worn on the rear, take the tire off and flip it around so the relatively fresh knobs on the other side get to play. Get to know the local sponsored pro riders because they probably change their tires often and you may be able to snag their lightly-used sneakers cheap.

10. Buy in quantity. Buy tires, oil, chain lube, chains, and other commodity products in bulk. Have a couple racing buddies split the cost with you and find a dealer who's willing to give you a discount if you buy oil by the case or a dozen tires at one time.

11. Never buy new. As much fun as it is to show up at the races with the latest and greatest ride, if you're bucks-down you need to buy used. What you want is a recent model that has seen only light use and (if you're lucky) has some of the good stuff (a pipe for example) added. A lot of motorcycles get purchased on a whim and then mostly sit in the garage. Sometimes illness, a lost job, a nagging wife, a kid on the way, or other life-changing

Publications, both print and online, pay small amounts for race reports. If you can string words together and take a few good photos, give it a try.

Volunteer to work at your local track.

circumstances are driving the sale. There are bargains to be found with some patient searching. You'll find the most used bike bargains at the end of the racing season or in the middle of a long, snowy winter. You can also find used riding gear online and in some bike shops.

12. Take care of your stuff. Neglect is expensive. Worn or misadjusted chains snap and destroy engine cases. Skipping oil or filter changes translates into shorter engine life and more expensive rebuilds. Dirty bikes hide problems that'll end up costing you more to fix. Abused bikes sell for less when it comes time to trade up.

If you're going to be wandering away from your pit area and there's nobody around to keep an eye on your things, slip a padlock through one of the disc brake holes. This will prevent the casual thief from rolling your treasured ride away.

A lap timer lets you accurately measure your speed each lap or through a particular section.

KEEP IT YOURS: SECURITY

There's no greater feeling of loss and violation than having your prized two-wheeled possession go missing. Think security both in the garage, on the road, and at the track by using good, tough locks and chains. Lock your bikes so they can't easily be moved or removed, whether they're in your garage, the back of your truck, or at the track. Get insurance to cover the bikes home and away.

At home: Run a thick cable or chain through the wheels and bike stand to keep it from being easily rolled away. Don't advertise the fact that you have bikes by leaving garage doors open, working on them in the driveway, or a decaled trailer.

At the track: Run a padlock through one of the discs or a cable lock through a wheel to keep it from being rolled off when you head for the concession stands or the riders' meeting. It only takes seconds to roll a bike into a van or trailer.

On the road: Lock it up, even if it's inside a trailer; and be sure to lock the trailer hitch! If it's in a pickup, have a big eye-bolt attached to the truck bed and run your locking cable/chain through it.

BUY A HELMET THAT FITS

Heads come not only in different sizes but also different shapes, either round or oval. That's why some brands of helmets will fit your noggin better than others. This is why you need to try on a variety of different brands and sizes at your dealer. What to look for:

- Style and color (yeah, might as well start with this since we all seem to be fashion slaves). Just as with girlfriends, don't fall in love with a specific helmet just because of how she looks or you may regret it.
- Confirm that it meets all the current rating standards; the labels inside will tell you. Snell and DOT are the stickers you want to see inside the helmet.
- Fit is easier to describe than it is to identify when you're trying it on. Some helmets will just seem to fit as if they used your head for a mold. Helmets should be comfortable but still snug, but without pressure points at your temples or forehead. With the strap buckled, shake your head hard, back and forth, and to the side. If the helmet shifts at all, it's too big and every time you land from a jump, the helmet will slam down and hit your goggles.
- Wear the helmet for a few minutes. If it starts to give you a headache, it's too tight.
- With the helmet fastened, lift up firmly on the rear of the helmet in an effort to roll it off your head in a forward direction. A correctly fitted helmet should not be able to be removed in this way.
- Bring along the goggles you use. Helmets vary quite a bit in how big the goggle port is and some goggles will barely fit or not fit comfortably. The time to find out is before buying the helmet.

Take your goggles along when shopping for a helmet as the eye ports on helmets differ quite a bit.

HOW TO TEST

Like most things in life, there are rules to testing the changes you've made to a bike. Here they are:

- Keep a logbook and write everything down. Memory is unreliable.
- Only change one thing at a time, otherwise you can't tell what the results mean.
- Know how things work (reading this book is a good start) and how they should work. You can't tell if a change is an improvement (or a mistake) unless you first know how it should be.
- Races may be the ultimate test, but never use a race as a test, at least if doing well in the race is your goal. Races are too chaotic to allow you to analyze your change(s) properly.

- Bring a knowledgeable friend and if the friend has a video camera, bring that too. Often someone standing by the side of the track can tell more about what the bike is doing than the rider can. Videotaping the bike at speed for later review on screen is how the pros do things. Camera images can be slowed down and studied.
- Buy one of the lap timers now available and use it to keep track of your lap times. DRC/Dirt Freak makes a $75 unit that's part of the crossbar pad and is easy to use.
- Keep the same lines. Pick lines you can hit consistently at a good hard pace. Consistency is essential in testing for the results to be useful.

Chapter 11
Mud, Sweat, and Gears: Race Day Problems and Situations

While I'll admit that my worst day riding is always more fun than my best day working, I know it's not always going to be perfect weather, a perfect track, and a stress-free day at the races. Dealing with the problems that the racing gods throw your way is part of the challenge. Here's some advice on coping.

MUD, SWEAT, AND TEARS

If you're going to be a serious rider, you have to learn how to survive and thrive on days when even the ducks are looking for shelter. Mud is a great equalizer, so learn how to use muddy conditions to your advantage. What to remember:

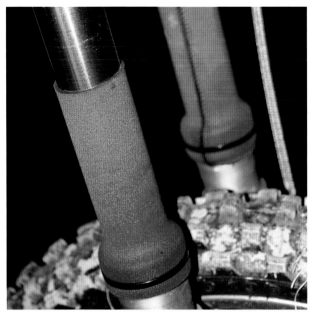

SealSavers are neoprene rubber booties that protect the fork seals from sand and mud. The down side is they increase fork stiction and are a bit of pain to put on (you have to drop each fork leg).

On muddy days, get to the start line early to get one of the drier (you hope) start positions.

Bike Setup

- Crank up the compression and rebound to compensate for the added weight of the mud.
- Reduce the race sag by 5 to 10mm for the same reason.
- Wet days are more humid so you would usually go leaner, but mud puts a strain on your motor, so you're actually better off going a little richer on the jetting.
- Spray WD-40 or Pam to the underside of fenders, your front number plate, skid plate, and anywhere else that you don't want mud to stick; reapply as necessary.
- Overheating is a problem when it's muddy. A strip or two of duct tape placed vertically on the radiator louvers will make them less likely to get caked with mud—the tape flexes enough to keep the mud from sticking.
- Another radiator trick is putting pantyhose over them. The thin nylon flexes and is hard for mud to get a grip on.
- Clean off mud between motos, whether this means using a power washer or just scraping it away. Take a run down an access road to throw any mud off the tires before going to the start line.
- Sharpen your pegs (you should be doing this anyhow) so your boots stay planted.
- Put closed cell foam in front of the skid plate and other nooks and crannies on the frame to keep mud from building up.
- Install a pair of handguards to keep muddy roost from getting on your grips.
- Check tire pressure and lower it to about 10 psi or less in the rear.
- SealSavers on your forks will keep wet, sandy mud from eating the seals. They're about $20 and come in a variety of colors. Good to have when it's muddy, you may not want them on all the time as it adds suspension stiction.
- Invest in an air filter cover designed for wet conditions. Twin Air makes a GP cover that fits over a regular filter to do a better job of keeping water out while not restricting airflow.
- Install a set of mud/sand tires. They make a big difference.

Personal Prep

- Install multiple tear-offs on your goggles or a Smith Roll-Off system (keep a pair of goggles in your gear bag with Roll-Offs already installed and ready for muddy practice laps or rainy days).
- Use an anti-fog product on the goggle lens. Scotts sells little anti-fog treated cloths that are easy to carry in your gear bag.
- Duct tape an old goggle lens over the end of your helmet visor. It helps keep roost off your goggles and if things get so bad you have to yank off your goggles, the old lens provides a way to look through your visor while ducking your head out of the muddy roost.

A holeshot device works by keeping the front end down and the rear end churning. However, it really only works with dirt start lines unless you get a special double-pin version.

- Carry along a pair of cheap plastic shop safety glasses. On really wet and miserable days, they'll work better than any pair of goggles and are also cheaper to throw away if necessary.
- Don't overdress. Just because it's raining and cool doesn't mean you should wear a raincoat or jacket. If you're warm and comfy while sitting on the start line waiting for your moto to start, you're overdressed.
- If possible, have someone come to the start line with an umbrella and your goggles in a plastic bag or wrapped in paper towels.
- Have a pair of grippy gloves in your gear bag. Cotton work gloves with rubber grip sections are available in any hardware store for a few dollars and help you hang onto wet handlebar grips. Or get a pair of waterproof gloves with a grippy section.
- Tuck a clean shop rag or small towel into the back of your riding pants. If you fall in the muck, use the towel to clean off your gloves and the grips.

Mucky Holeshots

- Holeshots are always good, but they're especially important when it's muddy. When you're the first rider at the first turn, you get to set the pace, and most important, don't experience browned-out vision and being showered with pounds of goop.
- Pick the gate with the straightest shot at the first turn unless it's a boggy mess. Tamp down and prepare the start as much as you can. On concrete starts, don't do a burnout; just spin the tire to clean it off.
- Bounce the gate a few times to make sure it's going to operate properly.
- Coming off the line, keep your weight back and keep your throttle action smooth to avoid going sideways in the slop.
- Aim for the inside line and guard it when you get there. Muddy tracks mean you'll be sliding more than usual, pushing the bike to the outside. It's going to drift wide whether you like it or not, so prepare for it.

A bent brake rotor will slow you down and make you nervous about your ability to stop. If you're lucky and careful, you can bend the warped section back to where it should be. See Chapter 3.

- Keep your weight back further than on a dry track. Use body english and plenty of throttle to steer with the rear wheel to get through the first turn because your front wheel won't be doing much of the work.
- If you didn't pull the holeshot, dive for the inside line anyhow. You may have to elbow your way in, but most of the pack is going to be sliding toward the outside of the turn. The inside line will get you out of most of the roost and the crashes caused by the muddy slides everybody's doing.

Mental Prep
- Many riders get ultra-cautious when things turn muddy. Wrong approach. Instead, use the mud to your advantage. Tell yourself you're going to have fun and that you and your gear are prepared, and then go do it. Knowing what to expect is half the battle, so before your moto, walk portions of the track that pose special problems—hills, some jumps, or especially boggy areas. Watch another class go through those areas, noting where the lines are and what the problems are going to be. If a spot looks like it could become a bottleneck, look for a shortcut around the problem area.
- Create your own lines, usually at the edges of the track where it'll be drier. Don't use the same deep rut that everybody else is using, as sooner or later—and it's always sooner—somebody is going to get stuck there and jam it up. You don't want to be the guy who's right behind him when he does it.
- Remember that the mud means the turns are slicker and the bike will tend to slide to the outside. Set up for turns expecting this and use it to your advantage.
- Keep your speed up; you don't want to lose momentum. The old saying of "when in doubt, gas it" is especially true when things get wet and ugly. Stay smooth on the throttle but also stay HARD on the throttle.
- Use roost to your advantage when passing. If you can throw up an especially nasty roost as you pass, it'll slow the other rider down like nothing else and you won't have to worry about him trying to get back past you. Use the roost!

STARTING ON DIRT VERSUS CONCRETE
Starting lines aren't created equal and it's smart to know what to expect when you roll up behind the gate.

Dirt
- The main risk is a wheelie if your body position is wrong or you're not aggressive enough.
- Wheelspin is a plus, not a minus, because it helps to keep the front wheel from coming up.
- Holeshot devices give you an advantage.
- Start with your body weight far forward and your head over the handlebars.
- Two-strokes are better out of the hole on dirt.

Concrete
- There's little chance of a wheelie.
- There's a big chance of spinning the rear tire and going nowhere fast.
- The usual holeshot devices don't work, although there are double-pin versions that don't hold the front end down as much.
- Coming out of the hole, concrete favors four-strokes.
- Start with your body weight centered on the bike.

WHEEL WON'T SPIN FREELY

If you have your bike up on the stand and notice that the wheel isn't spinning freely or it pulses when you use the brake, here are some possible causes:

- The brake rotor is bent (rocky roost or a crash will do that).
- The brake pad mounting pin is bent—take it out and see if it'll roll smoothly on a flat surface.
- One of the brake caliper mounting bolts is bent.

HEAD SHAKE

Head shake is scary. The front end oscillates violently under acceleration and a crash may be coming up. The quick fix is to slide your fork tubes DOWN in the triple clamps, which lengthens the forks and changes the head angle. You may also have too much air in the front tire or your forks may be too soft. The best fix, especially if this is a recurring problem, is to install a steering damper such as Scotts.

If you're getting head shake at speed on the track, the first thing you need to do is move the forks down in the triple clamps.

WARNING NOISES

- Popping: There's an air leak. Check to see whether your hot start trigger is actually opening and closing properly.

Also check the exhaust system, especially if it's an aftermarket unit. Is it letting air in?
- Clicking from the front wheel: If your front wheel clicks when you put the bike up on the stand, it's likely your steering stem nut is loose.
- Silence: Uh-oh . . . .

IT WON'T START

Without having to write a whole book on the two million possible reasons why a bike won't start, the short version is this: An engine requires four things in order to run: air, fuel, spark, and compression. Your initial job is to make sure those four things are present. Some tips:

- Assume you're an idiot. You did remember to take the rag out of the intake boot after cleaning the filter, didn't you? The filter is clean, isn't it? There's gas in the tank, right?
- Pull the plug and check that it's getting spark. A blue-white spark is what you want; yellow is bad and means you need at least a new plug.
- While you have the plug out, put your finger over the plug hole (if you can) and kick the bike through. Does it try to blow your finger off the hole? Then you have compression. If the kick starter moves through its stroke with little or no resistance, that's a clue that your top end is shot.

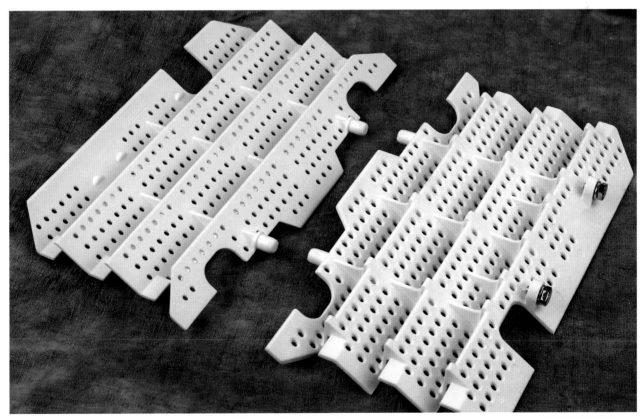

Radiator guards are there to protect the rads, not to move air. Drill additional holes to help air movement or purchase aftermarket versions peppered with openings like this.

Time for a soil sample!

- No spark at all? Could be the black box has gone bad. See if a friend or another rider with the same bike will let you borrow their black box, since they're easy to pop in and out of the bracket behind the number plate. If it starts with the borrowed black box, you'll need a new one as there are no fixes here.
- If you need a bump start, recruit one or two husky buddies and have them push you up to flank speed with the clutch in. Now pop it into either second or third gear (good for the big bikes) and let out the clutch. If the engine catches, ride around for a few minutes to warm it up. If this is a regular routine for you, start parking at the top of a hill.
- Hard starting in a four-stroke is a sign that the valves are out of spec. Adjust them.

THE RADIATOR IS MAKING LIKE OLD FAITHFUL

Overheating is common, especially with today's hot-running thumpers. Things you can do to reduce the geyser effect:

- Shut it down. Thumpers run hot and don't like to be left idling at the start line.
- Be sure the radiators aren't plugged or punctured—if you smell coolant, you'll already know you have a problem.
- Switch to a stiffer (higher psi) radiator cap to keep coolant in place.
- Install a recovery tank to collect coolant that would otherwise end up on the ground. The tank allows the coolant to be drawn back into the radiator when things cool off a bit. You may have to rig up your own system.

- Keep an eye on oil level and be sure you have the correct oil level at all times. Oil is a coolant as well as a lubricant.
- Make your water wetter by adding such products as Maxima Koolaide or Red Line WaterWetter.
- Be careful about installing massive radiator braces. Some designs, in their search for radiator salvation, actually reduce airflow.
- Be one with the wind. Lightspeed makes carbon fiber radiator wing extensions that funnel the breeze through the radiators more efficiently.
- Keep moving. Movement = airflow through the rads.
- Drill many small holes in the plastic radiator guards to let even more air through.

CRASH DAMAGE

Everybody crashes, from the multi-million-bucks factory pro to the lowliest novice. You could say it's the one thing we all have in common, no matter where we are on the moto food chain.

Crashes present their own style of race-day problems. Some post-impact quick fixes:

- The bars appear to be bent. Well, it's much tougher to bend today's aluminum bars, so they may not be. First, loosen the triple clamp bolts and see if it's actually the forks twisted in the clamps. Leverage things back into alignment and check your bars again.
- Still seem bent? It may be the bar mount in the triple clamp—the early Honda CRFs were especially prone to this part bending. There's no quick fix for this, just replacement, but at least you've saved yourself the expense of buying a new set of bars you don't need.
- A lever is now a stub. You have to have a clutch lever, so beg, buy, or borrow a replacement if you don't have a spare. Ask around in the pits as a lot of riders carry a spare lever—and after this, you will too. Tomorrow, invest in some ASV or similar folding levers. You can ride without a front brake lever, but you'll be slower than usual—or should be.
- A flapping piece of plastic fender or side panel can be stitched temporarily back into functionality with zip-ties.
- The throttle is sticking. Remove it from the bars, clean everything, and reinstall it, being sure it's not rubbing up against the end of the bar. If it's still sticking, you may have broken the plastic throttle tube and there is NO fix short of replacement. Never try and race with a sticking throttle—it's just not worth the risk.
- Broken spoke(s). Cut it off if you can; if not, zip-tie or tape the broken spoke to an unbroken spoke.

CHEAT SHEETZ® QUICK REFERENCE

GEARING

Countershaft	Changing 1 tooth on the C/S is equal to 3.5 teeth on the rear. Going from a 13/48 gear combo to a 12T C/S effectively makes the rear a 51.5T sprocket
Rear Sprocket	ADDING teeth = Gearing DOWN (lower top speed, quicker acceleration)
	FEWER teeth = Gearing UP (greater top speed, but slower acceleration)
Gear Ratio	Divide C/S sprocket teeth (e.g., 13) into rear sprocket teeth (e.g., 48). 48 divided by 13 = 3.69 gear ratio
	Gear ratio numbers go HIGHER as you gear down.

CARBURETION

Needle Clip	Moving the clip UP the jet needle makes it leaner.
	Moving the clip DOWN the jet needle makes it richer.
	The jet needle and its clip positions affect the carb's mid-range from 1/4 to 3/4 throttle.
Main Jet	The higher the number, the richer the main jet
	The main jet affects the carb's top-end from half to full open throttle.
Air Screw	Turning the air screw IN makes it leaner; OUT makes it richer.
	The air screw affects carb's idle to quarter-throttle range.
Lean Engine Signs	Poor acceleration
	Engine excessively hot or seizes
	Detonation and pinging
	Engine runs better when choke is applied
	Spark plug is white
Rich Engine Signs	Engine smokes heavily
	Worsens as it warms up
	Sluggish response to throttle
	Engine sounds dull and off-song
	Applying the choke makes it worse
	Spark plug is oily or fouls easily

JETTING AND WEATHER

Assumes your engine is jetted correctly for your altitude and normal (typical) conditions.

It gets colder	Engine runs leaner; Richen jetting
It gets warmer	Engine runs richer; Lean jetting
Humidity drops	Engine runs leaner; Richen jetting
Humidity increases	Engine runs richer; Lean out jetting
Higher Altitude	Engine runs richer; Lean out jetting
Hot, dry, and sandy	Engine works harder; go richer

TIRE PRESSURES

These are hot tire pressures, so if tires are cold, allow for pressure increase as you ride and the tire warms up.

Hard pack (blue groove)	14–15 psi
Sand	12–13 psi
Mud	10–12 psi (less if slimy mud; if tacky, go up so tires can spin and clean out the knobs better)

MUD, SWEAT, AND GEARS: RACE DAY PROBLEMS AND SITUATIONS

CHEAT SHEETZ® QUICK REFERENCE

METRICS

1 centimeter (cm)	0.394 inches
100 millimeters (mm)	4 inches (100mm is the most common sag setting)
1 meter (m)	3.281 feet
1 liter (l)	35.2 fluid ounces

SUSPENSION

Fork Springs	Measured in kilograms per millimeter or pounds per inch. Higher the number, the stiffer the spring
Shock Springs	Ditto. Higher = Stiffer

CONDITIONS

Mud	5/10mm LESS sag, stiffer on compression & rebound
Sand	5/10mm MORE sag, stiffer on rebound, maybe compression

SPARK PLUGS

Plug heat range	The higher the number, the cooler the plug temperature.
Plug Color	
White	Engine is running hot and lean
Brown	Properly jetted
Black and Oily	Running rich
Wet	Fouled and likely won't start

CHAPTER 12
Tips and Tricks

There are some things you only really learn by personal experience. Marriage and parenthood are two, racing is another. Nobody is likely to pay me for guidance on wedded bliss or raising kids, but I do know a lot about racing. Here are a selection of practical tips and tricks collected over the years from racing buddies, other riders, and sometimes hard experience. Some of this information is included in previous chapters but is repeated here for your convenience.

SAFETY WIRE UP TOP

Safety wire the throttle cable(s) to the throttle housing so they can't pop off in a crash or get snagged by a tree branch or someone else's handlebar in the first turn.

SQUEEZE IT IN

Many bikes have oil filler holes that are tiny or damn hard to get at. Filling them can be a chore. A simple solution is a large plastic squeeze bottle, especially if you can find one marked in 100ml graduations. Check your grocery store or the baby section at your local Megamart.

PLAN FOR THE BIG CRASH

Everybody crashes, and sooner or later you're going to auger in damn hard. If you're lucky, you'll crash where there's an emergency medical crew at hand or at least other riders who can get help. Plan ahead by making a copy of the label shown here. Fill in your personal information

Ashley Fiolek. *Simon Cudby/Throttle Jockey*

KNEE BRACE DAMAGE PREVENTION

Knee braces tend to wear through the knees of most riding pants quickly. One solution—other than buying your riding pants a dozen at a time—is to add some padding to the brace. Use either neoprene rubber or a piece of foam shin pad (you probably have a dozen of these lying around). Cut to fit and attach with zip-ties to the spot where the wear is coming from, being careful to not restrict the brace's movement. You'll probably have to replace this pad periodically, but it's cheaper than constantly buying new riding pants.

GET INSURANCE

New bikes are expensive, so insure them against theft, fire, flood, and other catastrophes (only getting ninth place doesn't count). Your insurance agent can quote you a plan to cover that expensive new two-wheeled possession, often as part of your current homeowner's insurance. Even vintage race bikes can be insured against loss—and they should be—although this may require an appraisal.

MARK YOUR CANS

If you have both two- and four-stroke bikes in the garage, use a permanent marker or spray paint to write "2" and "4" nice and big on the appropriate gas cans. Then there will never be any confusion as to which can holds the premix and which the straight gas. Make your riding buddies do the same to their gas cans so you don't accidentally grab the wrong one in the rush to get to the start line.

BEDPANS FOR OLD OIL

Need an inexpensive drain pan for oil changes? Plastic bedpans from a pharmacy or medical supply store are cheap and just the right size. Recycle the old oil by pouring it into sealed jugs and taking them to one of the oil-change places. Never just drain old oil into the ground where it pollutes the soil, leaves behind toxic metal compounds, and shows how ignorant you are.

YOUR SECRET STASH

To carry some cash while on a long trail ride or for a quick run to the concession stand, stash some bills inside the crossbar pad. In fact the crossbar pad is a good place to stick things like practice tokens, your race entry paperwork, or even a candy bar or power bar. Just carve out a niche in the foam to fit.

BLISTER PREVENTION

The best blister protection is simply to ride a lot. Strange as it sounds, you *want* to get blisters because blisters will eventually turn into hard callous. Wearing heavily padded gloves or taping your hands won't allow the tough callous that you need to develop. Wear thinner gloves, endure some early-season blisters, and let the callous develop naturally.

with a permanent marker. Stick it on the underside of your helmet visor and cover with clear packaging tape to protect it from the weather. The medics will see it when they take off your helmet. It's especially important to have this information on hand if you usually travel to the races solo. Now the emergency crews will know who you are, who to contact, and any existing medical conditions that might affect their treatment. (Don't know your blood type? Call up the Red Cross and schedule an appointment to donate blood, and they'll tell you then and you'll be doing a good thing for yourself and for others.)

CUT-OUT EMERGENCY INFORMATION LABEL

EMERGENCY INFORMATION

Name: _____

Emergency Phone #: _____

Age: _____ Blood Type: _____

Medical Conditions: _____

_____

RADIATOR HOSES THAT DON'T LEAK

With pretty much all dirt bikes now water-cooled, there's plenty of chance to spring a leak, especially with all the hose connections and clamps. When attaching and reattaching hoses, put a light coat of gasket sealer on the coolant fittings to make the hoses slide on easier and provide a better seal.

Dirt bikes are easy to steal and easy to resell or part out, since there's usually no title. Insure them. A vintage Maico bike like this is worth as much as a modern bike.

AVOIDING BLISTERS

Some simple steps to avoid blisters and ways to deal with blisters:

- Avoid new gloves on race day; they need to break in first.
- Have two or more pairs of gloves. When one gets wet, switch to a dry pair.
- Carry a needle in your car and an alcohol wipe so you can lance a blister that does form. This lets you keep on riding.
- Get gloves that fit. Forget brands or color coordination, you want gloves that are a snug and comfortable fit.
- If you have to tape your hands to ward off a blister, use sports tape and not adhesive or duct tape.

CHECKING THE OIL

With today's four-strokes, checking the oil level on race day is a must-do. But oil expands as it gets hot, so if you check the oil when the engine is cold, you won't be getting an accurate reading. Warm it up for a few minutes, then wait a few minutes after it's been shut off before checking the level. Some models are especially noted for rapid oil use (Honda CRF250 for one), so keep an eye on them. There's no excuse for an engine failure caused by too little oil because you were too lazy to check it regularly.

WET AND MUDDY VISION

On an ultra-wet and muddy race day, goggles have their limits, even with tear-offs and Roll-Off systems. Rather than ride goggle-less, have a cheap pair of safety glasses in your gear bag for days like this. Treat it with anti-fog (inside) and some Rain-X (outside) to prepare them for the elements. Because the safety glasses sit closer to your face and are more open, they're less likely to fog up or be affected by rain. Your eyes will have some protection from all the muddy roost, unlike all the other riders who are riding with bare-naked eyeballs.

MAKE A GOGGLE LENS LAST LONGER

Replacing a goggle lens is a pain and an expense. Roost eats them up and at $8 or so each (or more), it can get add up fast. One solution is to always run a tear-off over a new lens. Cut the tab off the tear-off and install. After your ride, remove it and install another.

BOOT WASHING

Wet boots take a long time to dry out and can get pretty funky. Buy a pair of tall warning cones like highway workers use—Home Depot has them. Put the boots upside down on top of each cone and wash them off. The cones keep the boots in place and because they're upside down, water is less likely to get inside. Stuff newspaper inside wet boots to help them dry out.

Riding a lot of classes with multiple gates? Can't remember if you're Gate 2 in Race 1 or the other way around? Write it down with a permanent marker on a piece of duct tape and stick it to your crossbar pad or gas tank. That way you don't have to trust the people working the start line to be sure you're lined up in the right class.

If you drain all the oil out of your bike to do some serious maintenance, use a Sharpie to write "No Oil" on a piece of duct tape or masking tape. Put the tape on your seat or gas tank as a reminder to keep you from absent-mindedly starting up and destroying an oil-free engine.

One of the things that is easiest to leave behind after a day riding is the triangle stand. I know, because I've found several that other riders left behind. The solution is to wrap some bright red or yellow duct tape around the stand. This will make it harder to overlook when you're loading up at the end of the day.

NEW BOOT BREAK-IN

Modern boots have more plastic than leather, which makes them even more rigid than before. Before you head for the track, do this:

- Put on your MX socks and walk around the house in the boots for a half hour or longer. This is the minimum break-in you should do.
- If the boots are still too stiff, run hot water over the leather portions, soaking them, and then put the boots back on again and flex them.
- Don't use power washers close to the boots as the high pressure will damage the leather, dyes, threads, and plastic.
- Let wet boots dry in the sun, lying on their side.
- Store boots lying on their side, not upright.

BROWN MUFFLER

If you notice a portion of your muffler has turned brown, it means the muffler packing has burnt out and a hot spot is developing. Repack it now because if you ignore it, it's possible the canister will break and you'll be buying a new one—and that's a lot more money than some muffler packing.

L'EGGS FOR YOUR BIKE

To keep mud from packing your radiators during really muddy races, put women's nylons over the radiators. Air will still flow through, but mud has a hard time sticking to the stretchy fabric. The nylons will be junk by the end of the race, but your sweetie can always buy you another set.

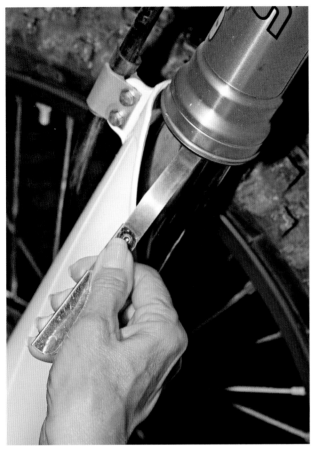

Your fork seals, that is. Seals typically leak because dirt gets past the wiper and seal. The grit sticks to the seal lip and the next thing you know, there's oil on the fork leg. When you see oil, pry the wiper down and stick a feeler gauge, old credit card, or a piece of stiff plastic such as the end of a zip-tie under the lip of the seal. Move it around the circumference of the seal to dislodge any dirt. Flush it out some more with spray cleaner or WD-40. If you catch this dirt soon enough, it can save you from having to buy new seals and wipers and the attendant hassle.

There are ways to remove dents from your pipes . . ..

REMOVING THE STICKY STUFF

Chain lube is intentionally pretty sticky stuff and that's bad news for anything the lube lands on that's not a chain. Spray some WD-40 on a rag and use it to wipe away the overspray, and if it still doesn't budge, switch to mineral spirits.

NO DUST GOGGLE LENS

Plastic goggle lenses are dust magnets. Try anti-static sprays or Armor All to cut the static and keep dust from clinging. Fabric softener dryer sheets are cheap, don't take up much room in your gear bag, and a quick swipe at the lens will give it an anti-static coating. If you're riding in an area with ultra-fine dust, tape over the foam on the top of the goggles or treat it with some baby oil.

GAS STAINS

Over time, gas fumes will yellow decals on tanks, or even the tank itself if it's not black. Put some household bleach on a rag and scrub the graphics or tank. The bleach will usually take out the yellow stains that gasoline and dirt leave behind.

NEVER USE GAS EXCEPT TO MOTO!

Never but never (and I mean NEVER!) use gasoline to clean parts, your hands, or your air filter. Gasoline is wicked stuff, filled with toxic multi-syllabic poisons. You don't want this poison on your skin. It's a suspected villain in some types of cancer, among other ailments. Gasoline will also eat through the adhesives in a foam air filter. Gasoline vapors are heavier than air, don't dissipate well, and any random spark can be enough to ignite them. The smart thing to do when handling gas outside the fuel can or tank is to wear nitrile or latex gloves and to immediately wash off any gas that gets on your skin.

DENT POPPING MADE SIMPLE

On both two-stroke and thumper pipes, you can remove a ding in a variety of ways, but the cheapest and simplest is to try freezing it out first. Take off the damaged pipe or section, fill with water, and place in the freezer so the expanding water has a place to go. The freezing action will drive out the ding, although you may have to repeat this process several times to get the results you want. But at least it's a cheap trick to try. Depending on the pipe and your freezer, you may have to cap or seal the pipe, but be careful with this as the force of water as it expands is stronger than you might think. Be careful you don't wreck the pipe in the process, and this tip works best on expansion chambers and thumper pipes that are a consistent diameter, but not ones with a FMF Powerbomb-type header.

SIMPLIFY REASSEMBLY

Save yourself time and lost fasteners. When you take something off, thread the fasteners a couple turns back into the holes they came from.

Handlebar weights can save your hands and arms some misery.

SOAK UP THE VIBES

On long off-road rides, your hands may go numb from the vibes. One fix is to install a set of road bike handlebar weights—they cost $10 to $20—and can be installed even if the bike has handguards or Bark Busters. ISDT and Dakar Rally riders often resort to this trick.

A THREESOME IS MORE FUN

When you need to carry three bikes in the back of a pickup, there are two ways to do it. Put two bikes strapped down as usual as far to side of the truck bed as possible. With the third bike, you can either back it into the truck (so it's facing the opposite direction from the other two) and run the tie-downs from the bars back, pulling the bike back to compress the suspension.

The alternative, especially if you have some type of front wheel chock and a pickup with a long enough bed, is to mount the middle wheel chock a foot or two further back from the ones on the sides. Just tie it down as usual in this case.

PLUGGING AWAY

Today's thumpers typically have spark plugs buried deep in the head. When installing a new plug, use a piece of fuel line over the end of the plug so you can safely lower it into place and get it started on the threads.

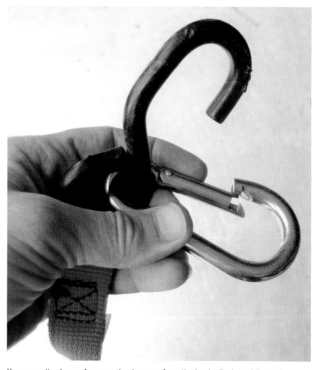

Keep your tie-downs from coming loose or from the hook slipping while you're trying to get the bikes in place by replacing the hooks with spring-loaded clips (carabiners) that climbers use to attach their ropes.

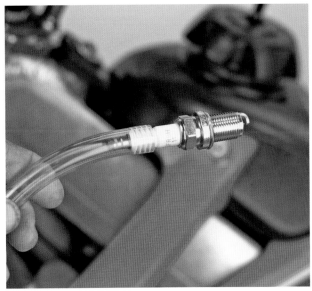

A piece of fuel line can make spark plug installation much easier.

A handful of plastic zip-ties can be used in an emergency to temporarily fix a flat tire so you can ride back to the truck. You can put two ties together to create a longer one that will wrap around the tire and wheel.

PLASTIC RIM LOCKS

Bring along some zip-ties. If you're unlucky enough to get a flat and don't have a repair kit along and it's a long hike back to the truck, use long zip ties (or link several shorter ones together) and wrap them around the tire and rim in as many places as you can. It's a good trick in an enduro where you need to stay on time and can't stop to fix a flat.

QUICKIE BRAKE BLEED

Brakes feeling spongy, but no time to do a proper bleed job? You can sometimes fix things by taking off the reservoir cap and then forcing the pads apart with a screwdriver. This forces fluid and the air (you hope) up the reservoir and out of the system.

STRIPPED THREADS

If you lightly strip out a small specialized screw or bolt—an oil level check screw, for example—try using some plumbing Teflon tape as a short-term fix. Wrap a few layers around the threaded portion and reinstall. It's not a permanent fix, but it will hold up long enough to get you through the day's ride.

KILL SWITCH MOUNTING

The two-piece brackets that some kill switches come with are annoying gimmicks and the mount screw is easy to lose. Toss it and feed a zip-tie through the slots on the switch, securing it tightly to the handlebar. If it rotates a bit, just slap a piece of tape on the zip-tie to hold it tight.

GET MAGNETIC

Use a magnetic mat to keep track of fasteners when working on your bike in the pits. Keep one in your race day toolbox as it folds flat and keeps you from losing that gotta-have-it screw on race day. Keep in mind, however, that not all the fasteners and spacers will be steel. No magnetic mat? Before starting work, spread out a shop rag where you'll be working and put each fastener on it so you can easily find them for reassembly.

Index